The Science of Sin

The
Science
of Sin

The Psychology of the Seven Deadlies

(And Why They Are So Good for You)

Simon M. Laham, PhD

THREE RIVERS PRESS
NEW YORK

Grateful acknowledgment is made to Brookings Institution Press for
permission to reprint an excerpt from *Economic Growth and Subjective
Well-Being: Reassessing the Easterlin Paradox*, Brookings Papers, Spring 2008 by
Betsey Stevenson and Justin Wolfers. Reprinted by permission of Brookings
Institution Press, Washington, DC, www.brookings.edu.

Library of Congress Cataloging-in-Publication Data

Laham, Simon M.
The science of sin : the psychology of the seven deadlies (and why they are so
good for you) / Simon Laham.—1st ed.
- p. cm.
Includes bibliographical references.
1. Pleasure.   2. Deadly sins—Psychology.   3. Vices—Psychological aspects.
I. Title.
BF515.L34 2012
150—dc23   2011017275

ISBN 978-0-307-71934-8
eISBN 978-0-307-71935-5

Printed in the United States of America

Book design by Lenny Henderson
Cover design by Jessica Bright
Cover photograph © Getty Images

1 3 5 7 9 10 8 6 4 2

First Edition

CONTENTS

Introduction

I confess it; I am a sinner. I greet most days with a mix of sloth and lust (which, coincidentally, is also how I end most days); this morphs into mild gluttony over breakfast and before I know it I've been condemned to hell several times over, and it's not even nine A.M. *Pride, greed, sloth, gluttony, lust, envy,* and *anger,* the seven deadly sins—these are my daily companions.

And you? Are you a sinner? Can you think of a single day in your life during which you didn't indulge in at least a few of these vices? I bet you can't.

The simple fact is that we all "sin," and we do it all the time. We lie and we cheat and we covet all manner of things, from our neighbors' wives to their bedroom suites. But fear not: The seven deadly sins aren't as bad for you as you might think. From gluttony to greed, to envy and lust, even these deadliest of vices can make you smart, successful, and happy. At least that's what I'll try to convince you of by the end of this book.

The seven deadly sins are ubiquitous. Geographer Thomas Vought, of Kansas State University, recently examined America's sinscape, mapping the sinful peaks and vice-filled valleys of counties across the United States.[1] Vought and his colleagues used statistics from different databases to compute sin indexes: violent crime stats to measure anger, prevalence rates of sexually transmitted infections to measure lust, and the number of fast-food chains per capita to measure gluttony. The basic message of Vought's research: the seven deadly sins are alive and well. Here, by the way, are the winners:

Most proud: Shreveport, Louisiana
Most greedy: Las Vegas Strip
Most slothful: Atlantic City, New Jersey
Most gluttonous: Tunica Co./Lula, Mississippi
Most lustful: Tunica Co./Lula, Mississippi
Most envious: Biloxi, Mississippi
Most angry: Shreveport, Louisiana

If everyone is indulging, why do the sins have such a bad name? Well, it's mostly the fault of Pope Gregory the Great. In his A.D. 590 book, *Morals on the Book of Job*, Gregory gave his short list for the deadliest sins.[2] He didn't invent the list, mind you; he simply refined previous efforts: those of the monks Evagrius Ponticus and John Cassian.

The deadly sins grew out of the monastic life of the early Middle Ages, when they were codified in an attempt to keep monks from running amok and quitting their spiritual calling. In short, the deadly sins were practical guidelines for maintaining the social order within ascetic communities. Monastic leaders didn't want a bunch of gluttons on their hands; there was, after all, not much food to go around. Neither did they want slothful, proud, or envious monks who would happily give up the hardships of the religious life as soon as they ran across a minor spiritual speed bump.[3]

The sins may have been codified in monasteries, but they have since been ingrained in the cultural consciousness of Western civilization. Pope Gregory's list established the deadly sins in the Western world as any but your run-of-the-mill transgressions.

Indulge anger or envy, and the penalty was not simply a slap on the wrist. These were serious offenses that could land you an eternity in hell. And this is what much of the Western world has thought about the seven deadly sins ever since. For centuries, the deadlies have exerted a powerful influence on the Western imagination, scaring the hell out of (or rather into) children and adults alike and infiltrating all corners of our culture, from the writings of Chaucer, Dante, and Milton to the movies of David Fincher.

In the psychological sciences, however, the concepts of sin and morality have quite a different history. Over the years, philosophers and scientists have made attempts to naturalize morality, stripping any divine gloss from the concept. Morality is now considered a set of evolved mechanisms that serve useful evolutionary ends.[4] As are the traditional "sins." In psychology, pride, lust, gluttony, greed, envy, sloth, and anger aren't considered "sins," or morally wrong, or even uniformly bad, but rather are complex and largely functional psychological states.

Each of the deadly sins does, of course, have its downsides, but each also has a range of positive, useful effects: anger breeds perseverance; sloth, helpfulness; greed, happiness; and envy can bolster self-esteem. In short, when it comes to the seven deadly sins, the picture is a complex one.

It is this complexity that I want to explore over the following seven chapters. The simplistic labeling of the seven deadly sins as "sins" or as uniformly wrong does nothing but breed contempt for "sinners" and stifle sophisticated discussion. This book rails against this kind of simplicity.

I have another confession to make: I am an experimental social psychologist. This means that I study human social behavior (especially moral behavior) by bringing people into the laboratory, manipulating some aspect of their thinking or action, and then watching what happens. This approach to studying behavior has proved fruitful in understanding much of what makes us tick. And it is this kind of work that forms the backbone of this book. Each chapter covers an array of psychological research that demonstrates the fascinating complexity of the seven deadly sins.

You may be thinking that people don't really consider the deadly sins as "sins" anymore. Well, let's not get ahead of ourselves. Many still take religious doctrines as quite literal guides for living.

Nevertheless, some of us probably don't consider eating too much or lazing around as prerequisites for entry to hell. The fact is, however, that the long cultural history of the seven deadlies *as sins* has left them with a grimy residue of negativity that is rather hard to wash off.

Consider the results of the following study.[5] William Hoverd, of the Victoria University of Wellington, and Chris Sibley, a psychologist at the University of Auckland, wanted to know whether people still think of sloth as immoral. To do this, they gave participants what's called an Implicit Association Test (IAT), a computer task designed to measure how closely two concepts are associated in the mind. Here's how the IAT works.

Imagine you're seated in front of a computer screen. On the left of the screen you see two category labels: "flowers" and "pleasant." On the right of the screen you see two more labels: "insects" and "unpleasant." Your task is to categorize target words that appear in the center of the screen into their appropriate categories by pressing a key with your left hand if the word belongs to a category on the left (flowers or pleasant) or with your right hand if the word belongs to a category on the right (insects or unpleasant). So the task proceeds: "Tulip" flashes on the screen and you press the left key, then "ugly" flashes up and you press the right key. These responses should be pretty straightforward. Because flowers and pleasant are quite closely associated in the mind (we all like flowers, right?), you should find it easy to respond to these categories using the same key. (The same goes for insects and unpleasant). The more strongly linked two concepts are, the easier it should be to respond to them when they form a single unit (i.e., are on the same key).

But now imagine that the pleasant and unpleasant category labels switch sides. Now you need to press the left key if the target word is either a flower or unpleasant and the right key if the target is an insect or pleasant. This should be much harder, as the paired categories (e.g., flowers and unpleasant) aren't very closely associated in your mind.

Hoverd and Sibley used the logic of the IAT to examine the strength of the association between "physically inactive" (akin to sloth) and "immoral." If people find it easy to respond to physically inactive and immoral when using the same key, then these concepts are closely associated; if they find it difficult, then these concepts aren't very closely related.

In the version of the IAT that Hoverd and Sibley used, on some trials physically inactive and immoral were paired on the same response key, and on others physically inactive and moral shared a key. Consistent with the notion that sloth is closely associated with immorality, people found it easier (i.e., they were faster) to respond to the physically inactive—immoral pairing.

The striking thing about the IAT is that it measures people's mental associations without their awareness. So what we have in Hoverd and Sibley's study is a demonstration of the powerful grip that the seven deadly sins have on our imaginations.

We may not consciously think that these sins are immoral, but their immorality is ingrained in us, embedded firmly within our unconscious minds.

In the face of such deeply rooted and powerful associations, these pages are also an exercise in old-fashioned rhetoric. I want to convince you that not only are the sins complex and interesting psychological states, but that, if indulged wisely, they are also largely functional and adaptive. To this end, I think you'll find the discoveries to come a remedy in an age in which even the most mundane of daily activities, from looking too longingly at the last cookie to kicking your feet up in front of the TV, are greeted with shame-inducing reproaches. This is not a manifesto for "all sin, all the time," but a reminder that far from leading us down the fiery path to hell, or even being generally dysfunctional, the seven deadly sins actually serve us quite well. So read on to discover why the greedy are happy, why the slothful are smart, why anger makes you a fearsome negotiator, and much more.

Now, where to begin? There is no definitive ordering of the deadly sins; each thinker on the matter has had his own preferred ranking system. I have been leaning heavily on Pope Gregory's list, so I'll go with his order. For Gregory the sins ranged in seriousness from the less insidious bodily sins up to the deadlier, spiritual ones: lust, gluttony, greed, sloth, anger, envy, pride.[6] Let's begin with the bodily and move to the spiritual. Let's begin with lust.

CHAPTER 1

Lust: Bras, Benevolence, and Better Grades

Clothes, rubber, shoes, glasses. This is not a shopping list. These are just some of the myriad and strange objects of lust. Fire and feet, trees and sheep also rate highly on some people's lists of things to do. Not just guys and girls, but animals, vegetables, and minerals of all shapes and sizes are objects of sexual desire. Of course, most of us lust after the regular brand of male or female, with no bells or whistles, no whips or chains or other attachments. But regardless of what turns us on, the *consequences* of being turned on are much the same.

Whether it's after Fred, Fiona, or Fido, when we lust we think differently and we act differently. And much of this thinking and acting is good for us.

As the sheer variety of lust objects suggests, this sin is a little more complex than you might think at first glance. We psychologists don't really use the term "lust," at least not often, in professional contexts or polite company. Rather, we talk of "activation of the sexual behavioral system." (I won't do this to you, however. So I'll substitute the simple "lust" for this mouthful.) Such activation consists of a complex of physiological reactions, cognitive and emotional responses, and behavioral changes. The main function of the sexual system, as you might expect, is reproduction. This, of course, doesn't mean that we have sex only to reproduce. In fact, according to a recent count, there are exactly 237 reasons why men and women have sex.[1] These include being drunk, wanting to get a promotion, celebrating a special occasion, and wanting to commune with God, as well as the more mundane wanting to feel loved and simply being horny.

Sex can fulfill these sorts of goals, but in evolutionary terms, the sexual system was designed to pass our genes to the next generation. And as you'll see, this system is remarkably well suited for that purpose. When we lust, a cascade of psychological and behavioral shifts is triggered, all aimed at increasing our chances of having sex and, as it turns out, doing much else besides. But before turning our attention to the benefits of lust, let's consider what this sin actually looks like.

What Do We Want?

"Women want love, closeness and someone who'll be a good father to their babies."[2]

"Place a glazed doughnut around your man's member, then gently nibble the pastry and lick the icing . . . as well as his manhood."[3]

According to men's and women's magazines, the sexes want slightly different things. And although *Men's Health* and *Cosmopolitan* might get the details wrong every now and again (personally, I prefer bagels), the sentiment is right: Men and women do lust after different things.

As for the human objects of lust, there are well-documented differences in what turns the sexes on. Heterosexual men typically want youth and beauty and waist-to-hip ratios of about 0.7.[4] Heterosexual women, on the other hand, are more often in the market for money, education, and status.[5]

One of the most interesting things about sex differences in lust is that we actually exploit them when seeking partners. We know what the opposite sex wants, and we play up those very qualities when we're out to impress.

We all do this. Think of the last time you went on a date. Men, did you try to look a little taller, darker, more handsome? And ladies, foundation for clearer skin? Black dress for that slimming effect?

When Jeffrey Hall of the University of Kansas surveyed the data from about five thousand users of online dating services, he found that both men and women were spot-on in their strategic misrepresentations: Men tended to bulk up their personal assets, pandering to women's desire for resources and status, whereas women tended to shave a few pounds off their weight. Both of these strategies make sense given the sexual preferences of the opposite sex.[6]

Now this might all seem terribly perverse: lying about one's wealth—shocking! But there is a sense in which we may not be able to help it.

James Roney of the University of Chicago induced lust in a group of young male students by exposing them to pictures of young women and then distributed surveys designed to regis-

ter changes in certain attitudes and preferences. He found that
after viewing such pictures, these students valued material wealth
much more than when shown pictures of older women.[7] These
lustful students also placed more value on ambition and status.
What seems to be happening here is that lust temporarily rejigs
our value systems. When sexually aroused we prefer and exag-
gerate qualities that increase our chances of sex; this happens
without our awareness. These lustful students weren't intentionally valuing ambition and wealth in order to impress; rather, lust
subtly penetrated and reconfigured their value systems in order
to give them a better chance of attracting mates.

Not only are the particulars of lust between the sexes different, but so too are more general attitudes toward the whole affair.
Stereotypes of the indiscriminate man, with a mind to hump anything with a heartbeat, and the more restrained, selective woman
both have a kernel of truth. In studies on sexual fantasies, men
often report a greater desire for variety than do women.[8] The
same pattern is seen in men's dreams, with multiple sex partners
appearing twice as frequently in men's as in women's dreamtime
dalliances.[9]

The most staggering demonstration that I know of men's in-
discriminateness and penchant for variety comes from one of the
finest field studies in social psychology.

In 1978 and in 1982, Russell Clark of Florida State University
and Elaine Hatfield of the University of Hawaii recruited a group
of twenty-two-year-old psychology students to serve as confederates (the term we use to describe experimenters' assistants or
stooges) in a study on gender differences in sexual attitudes and
behavior.[10]

Clark and Hatfield's stooges approached strangers of the

opposite sex at various places around campus. The confederates were advised to choose only those strangers they found attractive enough that they would actually sleep with them if given the chance. After scanning the crowd and selecting an appropriate sex-worthy candidate, the confederate would approach and say: "I have been noticing you around campus. I find you to be very attractive." After this less-than-smooth icebreaker, the confederate would continue: "Would you like to go out with me tonight?" or "Would you come over to my apartment tonight?" or "Would you go to bed with me tonight?"

In both 1978 and 1982, about 50 percent of participants, male and female, were happy to go on a date with a complete stranger. No gender difference here. But up the stakes a little, and women became somewhat reluctant. Only 6 percent of women were happy to go back to a strange man's apartment in 1978; none was in 1982. And a booty call? Not one woman in the sexually free '70s or early '80s was up for sex with a complete stranger.

The stats couldn't be more different for men. While 50 percent were happy with a date, 69 percent were up for an apartment visit and a healthy 75 percent (69 percent in 1982) were more than willing to head home with a woman for sex. If this last statistic doesn't count as a sex difference, I don't know what does.

Although these differences are striking and robust, there are of course similarities in the structure of lust. Both men and women are attracted to partners who are dependable, mature, kind, healthy, smart, educated, sociable, and interested in home and family.[11] And when surveyed about their reasons for having sex, men and women are remarkably similar: Twenty of the top twenty-five reasons given by men and women are identical.[12]

Sex differences in lust provide an interesting starting point for our exploration of this sin. Next, let's consider the similarities and differences in the effects of lust on the ways men and women think.

Sex on the Brain

As you might imagine, not all studies on lust can be done in the field. Researchers often turn to the laboratory to study sexual arousal and its consequences. And while the occasional experiment involves participants having sexual intercourse in an MRI scanner or having devices with names like "mercury-in-rubber strain gauge" or "vaginal photoplethysmograph" hooked up to various parts of their genitalia, most social psychologists are happy to resort to good old-fashioned priming techniques.[13] (More on priming next.) Typically, researchers show their lucky participants pictures of naked men and women, or words like *penis* and *orgasm*, and then wait to see what happens.

Take a study by Omri Gillath of the University of Kansas and his colleagues.[14] In this study participants completed what we call a lexical decision task, or LDT, which is used to measure the activation of concepts in the mind.

Here's how it works.

On each trial of an LDT, a string of letters flashes up on a computer screen and participants have to make a judgment about whether the letter string is a word or a nonword (i.e., they have to make a lexical decision). So on one trial you might see "hretea," to which you would hopefully respond "nonword" by pushing the appropriate button. On another trial, you might see "table," to which you would respond by pushing the "word" button. Of interest to researchers are reaction times to "word" responses—how long does it take you to deem "table" a word? The quicker the reaction time, the greater the activation of concepts related to the target word.

Things get particularly interesting in the LDT when "primes" are inserted between trials. Say, for example, that the word "chair" is flashed on screen briefly before "table." You're told to ignore the first word ("chair," called the *prime*) and respond with a lexical decision to the second letter string ("table," called the *target*). What happens here is that reaction times for judging "table" to be a word tend to be shorter after a "chair" prime than after a nonword prime (e.g., "ghjsj"). Why? It's about spreading activation in the associative networks that comprise our minds. The mind is a huge network of interconnected ideas and concepts. And when one concept in the network is activated (e.g., via presentation of the word "chair" in the LDT), this activation spreads to other, related concepts (e.g., "table") and thereby *primes* these concepts, making it easier to use them when needed.

Gillath, of course, wasn't interested in chairs and tables. He was more concerned with sex. But he used the same logic. Instead of words like "table," Gillath examined how long it took people to respond to target words such as "penis," "orgasm," and "intercourse." And instead of word primes, he used pictures of naked people of the opposite sex to the participant. What he found was that subjects were indeed faster to judge "penis," "intercourse," and other sex-related targets as words after being exposed to naked picture primes. (Even more fascinating is the fact that the primes used here were subliminal. They were presented for only thirty milliseconds, a time too short for participants to consciously register the content of the prime.) So exposure to sex cues triggers a spread of sex-concept activation across the associative networks of our minds, quite literally putting sex on the brain. But to what end?

What Gillath's study suggests is that thinking about sex (even nonconsciously) lowers our thresholds for perceiving sex-related information in the environment. In short, we start to see more and more cues as sexual. The most obvious advantage of this cognitive shift is that it increases our chances of having sex. Our basic cognitive functions become attuned to all things sexual, and this makes it more likely that we'll score.

The power of this mental shift becomes clearer when we consider some work by Jon Maner of Florida State University. In a fascinating series of studies, Maner primed undergraduate students with a "mating goal" (which is just a fancy way of saying he got students to think about sex).[15] He did this by showing a film clip in which an attractive man and woman get together and go on a romantic first date. After this he showed subjects photos of people of varying attractiveness. What he was interested in was participants' ratings of these photos for apparent expressions of sexual arousal. If lust is doing its job and gearing up the individual for sex, then we would expect that lust-primed participants would see sexual arousal in others, viewing others as potential mates. And this is basically what Maner found. Those who had sex on the brain after watching the romantic film read more sexual intent in the faces of others than did those in a control condition, who watched a thoroughly nonsexual documentary about people going up and down escalators. (The effect, however, was restricted to male participants who saw physically attractive targets.)

So on the whole, lust seems to be doing its job. It puts sex on the brain, which leads us to see sex in the environment, which, in turn, gives us the impression that the odds of having sex look pretty good. Other lust-induced cognitive shifts: we find other people more attractive when we're aroused and we pay more attention to physically attractive (i.e., sex-worthy) others.[16] In psych-speak: activated mating goals (triggered by exposure to naked pictures and the like) induce cognitive and behavioral strategies aimed at facilitating our reproductive success. In non-psych-speak: thinking about sex makes us think more about sex, which increases behaviors aimed at getting sex.

Sex and Trees

(Some people are sexually attracted to trees. This is called *dendrophilia*. This is not what this section is about.)

Lust is clearly good at triggering thinking and behavior that increase our chances of sex. But lust's implications for thought and action are far more wide-ranging.

One thing this sin does is focus attention on the immediate present. This of course makes sense given that lust is directed at a pressing current goal, namely, sex. It pays to focus our attention on stimuli in the immediate environment (usually people; sometimes clothes or rubber, or, yes, trees) that will fulfill the activated sex goal.

But this "present" focus that lust inspires is emblematic of a more generalized cognitive shift. Lust prompts us to place a premium not only on *sexual* stimuli in the present, but on other rewards as well.

Readers, I want you to do your best to get your hands on a bra. Go to your underwear drawer or to your partner's or use whatever other means are necessary. Now look at the bra. Feel the fabric. What do you think of the embroidery? The general craftsmanship?

Now, I want you to think about this choice:

> I can give you $15 right now or some other amount in one week. How much money would I have to give you in one week's time in order to dissuade you from accepting $15 right now?

When people are presented with such choices—choices between immediate and future rewards—they often prefer immediate rewards (even if such rewards have less value) and they require larger rewards in the future to give up those in the present.[17] This tendency to discount the value of the future is called future or delay discounting, but can also be thought of simply as impatience.

Although we all tend to discount the future to some extent, bra-handlers do it more. When men were asked the question above, those who had handled a bra required much more money a week later than did men who handled a none-too-sexy T-shirt.[18] (The study hasn't been done with women. I somehow doubt that men's underwear does the same thing.)

So just as lust ups the value of immediate sex-related cues, so too does it make the present seem much more valuable in monetary terms. And it's not just money, by the way. The same thing happens with candy and soda: Bra-handlers need more later to dissuade them from a certain amount now. The present is simply more valuable for the sexually aroused.[19]

But this *somewhat* general tendency to focus on and value the present may be part of an even *more* general attentional shift.

What letter do you see here?

H
H
H
H
H
H H H H H

An L or an H? Of course you can see both, but what if I asked
you, "Do you see an L?" or "Do you see an H?" and had you answer
as quickly as possible? When psychologists ask participants to do
exactly this, they find intriguing differences in how long it takes
people to respond.

Why? Because of differences in what's called global versus
local processing. Global processing is all about the big picture;
it's holistic, it takes the long view, it sees the forest rather than
the trees. In the L versus H example, global processing is quicker
to see the forest L than the little, tree Hs. Local processing, on
the other hand, is all about the details; trees not forests; Hs, not
Ls. There are a number of things that trigger global versus local
processing. For example, people from East Asian cultures tend to
be global processors, whereas those from the West tend to be local
processors.[20]

Now, it makes sense that if lust narrows our *temporal* attention
to the here and now, it might also narrow other dimensions of attention, leading to detail-oriented, local processing.

To test this possibility, Jens Förster, a social psychologist
from the University of Jena, Germany, and his colleagues, Amina
Özelsel and Kai Epstude, primed participants with lust by having

them think about casual sex with an attractive partner and then gave them a series of composite letter stimuli like the one above.[21] And just as you would expect if lust triggers local processing, participants were faster to say they saw the "tree" letters (i.e., H in the example) than they were to say they saw the "forest" letter (L). Lust is local, not just in time, but in general processing terms. It's about working out the details of where to put what, in which order.

But what good comes of this kind of lust-induced processing? Well, local processing is linked to what psychologists call analytic thinking. This is the kind of thinking involved in solving problems like: "If A is less than B and C is greater than B, then is A less than C?" which are in fact part of the Graduate Record Examination and other academic tests. To get the answer here, as in other analytic problems, one has to reason logically and often laboriously from a set of facts. One has to build one's answer from the details up.

When Förster and colleagues, in another study, again primed participants with sex and gave them a series of analytic thinking problems, they found that these lustful reasoners solved about three problems over the course of a four-minute testing period, one more, on average, than control subjects.[22]

The moral of all this: just before your next exam, watch porn.

The Lustful Nonconformist

About one-fifth of advertising uses sex to sell its products. It's a fair assumption that sex sells. Put a sexy woman next to a packet of gum and one might expect the positive qualities of the woman to rub off on the gum, making it seem more appealing. This all makes intuitive sense and is in fact based on sound psychological theorizing about what's called "evaluative conditioning." (This is simply the idea that when a positive stimulus is consistently paired with a neutral stimulus, the neutral stimulus comes to be judged more positively. The same logic holds for pairing negative and neutral stimuli: Neutral becomes negative.)

But the real problem here is that the evidence suggests that sex doesn't really help sell much at all. Even though most people do find sex a generally positive concept (although women often have mixed feelings about it), sexual stimuli are also quite distracting.[23] And so embedding a product in a sexual context often leads to poorer memory for the product, which is not what an advertiser wants, given that brand memory is a key predictor of purchase intentions.[24]

Sex doesn't seem to work in advertising and doesn't seem to work in film, either. When Anemone Ceeridwen and Dean Simonton looked at the box office performance of 914 films released between 2001 and 2005, they found that the sexual content of a film was actually negatively correlated with box office grosses (that is, more sex, less money).[25] What does predict box office success? Despite the hope of most directors and producers that it's the artistic integrity of their work that draws in the dollars, a film's early grosses are actually best predicted by the number of screens it's released to.

But I want to try to salvage something from the sex-sells mantra, before we dispense with this time-honored but apparently false bit of advertising folk wisdom altogether. Bear with me on this, it's a rather circuitous route.

In a fascinating piece of empirical work, Vladas Griskevicius, a psychologist at the University of Minnesota, and a group of his colleagues considered how lust might influence the way people conform.[26]

We often conform to, or go along with, the behavior of others for two basic reasons: one, to be better informed (if you are unsure of what to think or do, it is often a good bet to think or do what others think or do), and two, to be liked or to fit in. Usually, these motives are functional, and so conformity serves us well. But there are times, Griskevicius reasoned, when following the status quo isn't very useful. There are times when it's better to stand out than blend in. And one of these times is when we're in the mood for sex.

In the sexual marketplace we are vying for the affections of a buyer, so we need to tout our unique wares and communicate some kind of competitive advantage. And if standing out can lead to being seen in a positive light, then lust should actually decrease our tendency to conform.

Following this logic, Griskevicius designed a series of studies to test the effects of sex-priming on conformity. The details of the results are a little complicated, but the gist is straightforward: Lustful men became nonconformists when standing out was sure to convey a positive self-image. Women value traits like decisiveness and independence in their mates, and nonconformity is a way for men to signal these qualities. The story for women is a little different. Sex-primed women, in Griskevicius's study, were actually *more* likely to conform if such conformity signaled a positive image to potential mates; this is explained by men's preference for agreeableness and affiliation in a mate. When sexually aroused, women sought to convey their affability by going along with the group.

So what does any of this have to do with sex in advertising? Well, if sex is to be used wisely, it seems that it should be used only in selling products that promote uniqueness in men or conformity in women. If men see a half-naked woman standing next to a watch that is meant to make them unique, then we might have a successful ad campaign on our hands. If she's holding up a shirt that won't distinguish its wearer in any way from a multitude of other wearers of similar shirts, then we might have a problem. For ads targeted at women, however, the opposite may be true.

The Lustful Samaritan

I was never very good at extracting the point of parables in Sunday school: I found the whole exercise tedious and I was always confused about why so much of ethics was founded on the unsuccessful sowing of seeds and similar agricultural futilities. Still, even for my literal brain, the parable of the Good Samaritan was an easy one. Here it is, paraphrased:

> A guy gets beaten up and is pretty much left for dead on the road from Jerusalem to Jericho. As he lies on the roadside, he is passed by a priest and a Levite (also a religious functionary) who fail to offer any help. But a passing Samaritan stops and helps, bandaging the man's wounds and taking him to an inn.

A question that's not often asked about this parable: What would have happened if the priest and Levite were horny?

In an interesting series of studies, again by Vladas Griskevicius, heterosexual men and women were shown pictures of attractive members of the opposite sex and were then asked to imagine going on a date with the one they liked most.[27] After this task had put them in a lustful frame of mind, they indicated their willingness to offer help in a variety of situations:

- Would you donate money to natural disaster victims at a booth on campus?
- Would you distract a grizzly bear that was attacking a stranger?
- Would you volunteer to go to Washington, D.C., to help coordinate meetings between charities and White House officials?
- Would you give a speech for a good cause to a large and potentially hostile crowd?

How would lust influence one's proclivity for these kinds of prosocial behaviors? Remember that lust's function is to increase the chances of having sex. One way to do this is by boosting our overall attractiveness to potential mates. And a fairly good strategy for increasing attractiveness is to communicate valued qualities.

When it comes to personality, men, remember, tend to value prosocial qualities in women: agreeableness and affiliation. So one might expect that lustful females, recognizing that men like helpful, agreeable women, might do everything they can to show off their generosity. And this is what Griskevicius found: Across most of the helping questions asked, lustful women said they'd help more than did the nonlustful.

Now for men, the story is a little more complicated, but it still makes sense. Although women do value prosociality in men, they also value a potentially competing quality: dominance. Given this trade-off, it makes sense that men would help in only those situations that communicate *both* of these valued traits. And this is what we see in Griskevicius's study.

If you take another look at the helping questions, you'll notice something interesting. Some of them involve clear opportunities both to help *and* to demonstrate heroism (grizzly bear distraction), prestige (going to the White House), and dominance (staring down an angry mob). And just as Griskevicius expected, lust triggered helping for men only in these situations, ones in which the act of helping also indicated prestige, leadership, or heroism. Women like helpful heroes, and so lustful men took the opportunity to display their helpful heroism.

So once again we see lust promoting behaviors that increase the likelihood of sex. Women like men with status and prestige, and, sensibly, lust encourages men never to miss an opportunity to convey these qualities. Men like agreeable girls, and so behaviors signaling such qualities are triggered in lustful women.[28] It just so happens that in this case, the behaviors triggered by lust benefit not only lustful individuals themselves, but also those around them.

As for the Levite and priest . . . well, had they been aroused and had the injured man been under attack by a grizzly bear . . . who knows?

Although much of what lust does is directed at the present, this sin also seems to have the good sense to realize that sometimes getting someone into bed takes a little time. Men can't expect simply to dance around in front of a bear and have random women fall willingly into the sack. So while lust does initiate cognitive and behavioral shifts that increase our chances of *immediate* sexual fulfillment, it also triggers other processes aimed at increasing our chances of sexual success in the long run.

Take a moment and think of four things that are really important to you. Four things, that is, besides any romantic relationship you happen to be in at the moment. Family perhaps? Or work? What about your hobbies or your DVD collection?

Now I want you to answer this question for each of these four things:

> Imagine that it's not possible to engage in _____ [insert your four important things here, one a time] and still maintain a relationship with your partner. In this case, would you consider ending your relationship in order to continue doing _____?

This is a modified version of what's called the "willingness to sacrifice" questionnaire, which is used to gauge people's tendency to suspend one's own interests for those of a romantic partner. Obviously, the less willing you are to end the relationship, the more you value your partner.

When Omri Gillath, who did the LDT priming study outlined earlier, and his colleagues gave a test like this to lust-primed subjects, he found that these people were more willing to make sacrifices for their partners than those exposed to neutral primes.[29] In similar studies, he found that lust also triggered other pro-relationship behaviors: more willingness to share information about oneself with a partner and more accessible thoughts about intimacy.[30] And when sex-primed participants were given a number of options to pursue in hypothetical relationship conflict scenarios, they tended to opt for positive, constructive resolution strategies rather than negative, destructive ones.

Essentially what we have here is lust triggering what are traditionally considered love-related thoughts: sharing, intimacy, and so on. Each of these effects is an example, argues Gillath, of the lust system pursuing short-term goals that increase the chances of our getting sex in the longer run. If we have a relationship and can maintain it by communicating, focusing on intimacy, and adaptively resolving conflict, then we have a greater chance of having sex and reproducing. Love functions here in the service of lust.

Lust, Caution

Of course, it's not all good news when it comes to lust.

Dan Ariely, who was at MIT at the time, and George Loewenstein, of Carnegie Mellon University, were interested in young men's judgments about sexual stimuli, risk taking, and sexually coercive behavior.[31] These researchers gave each participant in a study a specially designed laptop to take home. Each computer had a modified keypad designed to be used easily with one's non-dominant hand. (This should give you a hint about what's coming next.)

Some participants simply took the computer home, opened up the experimental program, and answered questions like these:

- Are women's shoes erotic?
- Can you imagine getting sexually excited by contact with an animal?
- Is a woman sexy when she's sweating?

These questions were all about what turns men on. Other questions tried to get at the lengths one would go to in order to have sex:

- Would you slip a woman a drug to increase the chances that she would have sex with you?

And yet others measured beliefs and attitudes about unsafe sexual practices:

• Would you use a condom if you didn't know the sexual history of a new sexual partner?

While some participants simply answered these questions at their leisure, others were asked to answer them while they viewed erotic pictures and masturbated. To these participants, the computer program presented not only the questions to be answered, but also pictures of naked women and an "arousal thermometer" that participants could use to track their lust levels. The researchers wanted these lustful participants to be in a "high but sub-orgasmic" state before answering the questions, so they were instructed to answer only when their arousal levels hit 75 degrees on the arousal thermometer. (This 75-degree mark was deemed high enough to indicate sufficient arousal, but not too high to place participants in danger of ejaculating. God knows how this criterion was calculated.)

What was of particular interest to Ariely and Loewenstein was how sexual arousal would influence these young men's answers. The results are striking. Lustful participants were much more likely to find a range of stimuli and behaviors exciting compared to their nonmasturbating peers: Shoes were more erotic, as was urination, anal sex, sweat, cigarette smoking, and twelve-year-old (and indeed sixty-year-old) females. What's more, lust increased men's willingness to drug a woman for sex, lie to get her into bed, and—I suppose this isn't so bad—take her to a fancy restaurant. Even men's beliefs about the safety of sexual practices seemed to change with lust: Masturbators were more likely to think that birth control was the woman's responsibility and that condoms decrease pleasure and interfere with spontaneity.

This general lust-inspired risky shift can occur even without the whole masturbation part. The mere presence of an attractive woman may be enough to make men do some pretty stupid stuff, as another study shows.

Richard Ronay and Bill von Hippel, both at the University of Queensland, sent some researchers to local skateboard parks in Brisbane, Australia, to recruit male skateboarders for participation in a study.[32] The skateboarders were asked to choose one easy and one difficult skateboarding trick and were then filmed while attempting each trick ten times. The key factor in the study was the sex of the researcher: Some skateboarders tried their tricks in front of a male experimenter and others in front of an attractive female experimenter. Ronay and von Hippel were interested in just how hard these skateboarders would try to impress the experimenters.

When skateboarders try a difficult move, there is a split second in which they must decide whether to abort the trick in order to avoid injury, or risk landing it. What Ronay and von Hippel expected was that these brave young skateboarders would be a whole lot braver in front of attractive women than in front of men. And this is exactly what they found: Skateboarders were more likely to risk landing a difficult trick in front of an attractive female than in front of a male. Although this riskiness did result in more crash landings, it also resulted in more successful trick completions.

The results of these studies are reasonably straightforward: When lustful (or in the presence of a potential mate), men are more willing to do a lot of silly, risky things. Of course, sometimes the risk pays off in terms of increasing the likelihood of sex: It may help them stand out among competitors or lead them down sexual avenues they wouldn't otherwise have taken. But sex clearly is not the only thing at stake here; it is one good among many. And when lust-fueled skateboarding lands us on our heads or elbows, or when sexual arousal predisposes us to coercion or worse, we know that lust has served us ill.

The Human Peacock's Tail

Much of the discussion thus far has hinted at the evolutionary function of lust. Feelings of sexual arousal trigger thoughts and behaviors aimed at sex, and it is, of course, through sex that we pass on our genes. From the evolutionary point of view, anything that makes us more likely to survive and reproduce (and is heritable) has a good chance of being selected. Thus lust is an evolved psychological mechanism (an adaptation) aimed at reproduction. Pretty straightforward.

But there's another and more interesting account of the lust-evolution link, one that flips this reasoning on its head. And at the heart of this thesis is a rather challenging idea: that lust is not merely an adaptation, a simple product of evolution, but rather a force that actually *drives* evolution—a force that may in fact account for much of what is interesting about humankind, including art and music, theatre and sport, and even language. The thinking on this issue begins with the strange case of the peacock's tail.

Peacocks, as you're probably well aware, have big, bright, and quite spectacular tails. But have you ever asked yourself why? What is the use of such extravagant plumage? From an evolutionary point of view, such a tail seems puzzling at first glance: A peacock could still technically mate with a peahen even if he had a smaller tail, and from the survival angle, a large, cumbersome, multicolored advertisement to predators is hardly a good investment.

So why do peacocks have such seemingly disadvantageous tails? Ornaments like the peacock's tail evolve because they provide an advantage not in terms of survival but in terms of attractiveness to the opposite sex. Because peahens are rather choosy (in fact, females of most species are choosier than males), peacocks have to compete for their affections. And because peahens have a thing for big tails, such an extravagance proves an advantage in the mating market.

The process by which such ornaments come to evolve is known as sexual selection, which maintains that certain aspects of behavior and appearance have evolved not for survival benefits but because they help attract the most or the best mates. Sexual selection is thought to be responsible not just for the peacock's tail, but for ornamental characteristics of other species as well. In fact, evolutionary psychologist Geoffrey Miller of the London School of Economics suggests that it may be responsible for the ornamental aspects of human nature.[33] For Miller, things like art, music, and theatre, which don't seem to offer much in terms of survival benefits, may make us more attractive to potential mates. These qualities are the human equivalent of peacocks' tails. We flaunt our intellectual, artistic, and sporting prowess much like the peacock flaunts his tail, and potential mates choose us based on these qualities. This remains a controversial idea, but there is some work that supports it.

Take the case of creativity. Although some have speculated about the survival benefits of the creative instinct (e.g., creative fishing techniques bring in more fish), others have questioned such survival-based explanations. Although creative fishing or hunting techniques might prove useful for survival, what is the good of the creativity of poetry or song? It's unlikely that such creative devices can be used to charm fish out of the ocean or big game onto one's spear.

Creativity, like other human ornaments, Miller argues, is not for survival but for attracting mates. For Miller's argument to work, we should expect creativity, like other ornaments, to have certain properties. First, we should expect people to find creativity sexually attractive. And, good news for Miller, humans do prefer creative types as mates.[34]

We should also expect people to *display* creativity when they have the opportunity to attract a mate. Earlier we discussed the idea that people know what the opposite sex wants, and so, when in a lustful state, are likely to flaunt such desired traits. The same holds for creativity. When Vladas Griskevicius primed participants with lust by having them imagine going on a date with an attractive, desirable romantic partner, he found participants were subsequently more creative when asked to write a story.[35] When thinking about a potential desirable partner, the ornament of creativity was put on show.

Creativity is not the only, or even the most interesting, human ornament. One of the most provocative aspects of Miller's thesis is that moral virtues may also function like the peacock's tail. In essence, Miller suggests that lust could actually be responsible for the evolution of virtue. And in more good news for his account, research shows that people do find virtuous traits like kindness, empathy, and honesty sexually attractive.[36] Moreover, the work by Griskevicius on the impact of lust on helping, discussed a few pages back, shows that when in a lustful mind-set, people are indeed more likely to help, especially if such helping conveys valued qualities to potential mates.[37] Miller's thesis is, as I mentioned, controversial, but lust's status as a sin does seem on rather shaky ground if it is actually responsible for much of human virtue.

When it comes down to it, for many, the real problem with lust is that it may lead to sex or, God forbid, masturbation, the latter of which the Catholic Church, as recently as 1994, condemned as an "intrinsically and gravely disordered action."[38] The virtues of sex and masturbation, lust's behavioral bedfellows, are too numerous and varied to go into here and are beyond the scope of our current concerns anyway. Our focus has been lust, the psychological precursor to sexual activity. And in looking merely at this sin, I hope you have been convinced that it is in fact far from all bad. The lustful mind-set is functional, and it can promote benevolence and creativity and even higher GRE scores under the right conditions. This deadly sin, much like the other six, is far from disordered—intrinsically, gravely, or otherwise.

CHAPTER 2

Gluttony: Eat, Drink, and Be Merry, Smart, and Helpful

I f Pope Gregory the Great had it right, the French are going straight to hell. Gregory wasn't anti-French per se; it's just that the portrait of the glutton drawn in his *Morals on the Book of Job* bears some resemblance to the modern Frenchman. Gregory made it impossible to gain any pleasure at all out of eating when he listed not one, but five ways to sin by gluttony. We have the obvious "too greedily" and "too much," but we also have less straightforwardly condemnable modes of eating: "too early," "too expensively," and "with too much focus on how the food is prepared."

This multidimensional, Gregorian brand of gluttony looks very much like the modern French attitude toward food. In a world in which many of us are especially concerned with the nutritional aspects of what we eat—high GI or low, good fat or bad—the French have a refreshingly insouciant attitude toward the culinary, an attitude that revolves around the pleasures and experience of eating.[1] Although refreshing now, this pleasure-maximizing attitude toward food was anathema in those Middle Ages monasteries in which the deadly sins were codified. When gluttony was deemed deadly in the Middle Ages, pleasurable overindulgence in food and drink spoke of an ungodly preoccupation with earthly, bodily pleasures, which came at the expense of a more proper focus on the divine and spiritual.

These days, of course, gluttony is no longer the multiheaded beast that Gregory described and condemned. Now gluttony is one-dimensional; it is all about eating *too much* and is moralized because of its link to obesity. For many, "gluttony" is synonymous with "fat." The good news for the French, however, is that on this contemporary gluttony = obesity account, it's the Americans, not the French, who are on their way to hell. For despite its gluttonous attitude to food, France has a lower prevalence of obesity than the United States.[2]

Of course, gluttony and obesity aren't the same thing. Even if we constrain ourselves to the "eating too much" definition of the sin, it's clear that gluttony is a *manner* of eating, whereas obesity is a condition of the body defined technically as a body mass index greater than 30. (It's also interesting to note that when "eating too much" was first added to the list of sins, it had nothing to do with being fat. It was taking pleasure in the excesses of food that was the sin, not an expansive BMI.)[3]

Although this chapter is about the many forms of *gluttony* (and not obesity), the connection between the two is so tightly drawn in the modern world that I would be remiss not to say a few words on the gluttony-obesity link.

Many people attribute obesity and being overweight to the gluttonous impulses and moral failings of the individual. People who regularly eat burgers, fries, and double-fudge ice cream sundaes are seen as more unethical and inconsiderate than those who eat fruit and salad.[4] The overweight are judged to be morally corrupt consumers of toxic junk, lazy and lacking in self-discipline.[5]

But blaming obesity on the moral failings of the gluttonous individual is counterproductive for at least two reasons. First, in moralizing fat, one stigmatizes the obese and overweight, which not only makes life less than pleasant for these individuals, but also increases the tendency to overeat, thereby compounding the problem.[6]

The second issue with attributing obesity to mere gluttony is that it overlooks the critical role that the environment plays in shaping how, what, and how much we eat.

Social psychologists have long known that human behavior of all kinds is at the mercy of the environment. Eating is no exception. The relationship between the gluttonous drive to consume and its impact on the body depends crucially on one's surroundings. Put simply: gluttony is adaptive in environments in which calories are scarce (like the African savannas of our deep evolutionary history) but not in those in which calories are plentiful (like Mississippi). The desire to eat and eat a lot is what kept humans alive and healthy enough to reproduce in the relatively food-impoverished conditions of our evolutionary past. We evolved to eat much and do little, a sensible strategy when calories are hard won. In evolutionary terms, gluttons survived; dieters did not.

But gluttony looks a little different in the contemporary industrialized Western world. Because of an abundance of convenient calories in our environment, our evolved drive to rampantly consume has become maladaptive. The real problem is not gluttony per se, but gluttony in the midst of the caloric excesses of McDonald's, KFC, and Stouffer's frozen microwavable dinners. When calories are hard to come by, an insatiable appetite is an insurance policy, an adaptive motivation that helps one pack away a few extra pounds for a rainy and food-scarce day. But when the same basic drive can be satisfied with a short trip from the couch to the plentifully stocked fridge, the gluttonous urge to consume sets us off on the path to obesity.

The role of the environment in consumption is difficult to overstate. Take the simple environmental cue of portion size.

Brian Wansink, a food researcher at Cornell University, has spent a considerable amount of time studying the impact of serving sizes on eating habits. Time and again he has shown that the amount of food one is served determines the amount of food one eats. People given a one-pound bag of M&Ms eat about twice as many as those given a half-pound bag; moviegoers given large servings of popcorn eat about ten grams more than those given medium servings.[7] More generally: double the size of a meal, and you'll eat up to 25 percent more; double the size of a snack, and you'll consume up to 45 percent more.[8]

Portion sizes sway our eating habits for a couple of reasons. First, serving sizes indicate consumption norms. They say, "This is how much most people are eating; this is what is normal and appropriate."

But serving sizes also drive consumption because of what Wansink calls the "clean the plate" phenomenon. Somewhat counterintuitively, we stop eating not when we're full, but when the plate in front of us is empty. If the plate isn't empty, we won't stop eating.

In one beautifully devious study, Wansink and a couple of his colleagues brought students into their lab for a "soup-only lunch."[9] After being seated in groups of four, these students were told that they would be eating tomato soup, a new recipe, and they were encouraged to eat as much as they liked. About twenty minutes later they completed a questionnaire asking them what they thought of the soup, how much they thought they ate, and other, similar questions. What Wansink was interested in was how much soup these participants ate. And he found something quite interesting: Some participants were consistently eating about 75 percent more soup than others.

Why? What was so special about these apparent soup lovers?

Well, here's the devious part. Even though all of the students were eating out of what *appeared* to be identical bowls, some bowls were in fact "bottomless." Wansink had rigged some of the bowls to be self-refilling. Unbeknownst to participants, two of the bowls at every sitting were connected via a hidden tube to large pots of soup concealed beneath the table. Wansink had created an elaborate filling and drainage system, which ensured that, as participants ate, the bowl would imperceptibly refill.

What Wansink was doing was manipulating the clean-the-plate phenomenon. Some participants were able to clean their plates while others were prevented from doing so by Wansink's refilling system. And it was the latter participants who ate much more. These unwitting soup lovers gorged themselves not because they were hungrier, not because they were obsessed with tomato soup, but because they never saw the bottom of their bowls.

But portion size is not the only environmental cue that messes with our eating habits.

Here's a question: From which glass shape do you think you'd drink more—the highball on the left, or the tumbler on the right?

Most people think they'd consume more out of the highball, but most actually drink more out of the shorter, wider tumbler.[10] Because we place undue emphasis on the vertical dimension of things (at the expense of the horizontal), height looms larger than width in our judgments. Undue emphasis on the height of these glasses makes us think that we'd consume more out of the taller highball.

The list of subtle environmental shapers goes on: We dish out and eat more ice cream from 34-ounce compared to 17-ounce bowls; we eat more Hershey's Kisses if they're in a transparent rather than a white bowl; and we eat more M&Ms if we have ten rather than seven colors to choose from.[11]

Despite the pervasiveness and potency of such environmental factors, much of this influence is outside of our awareness. We simply don't appreciate the fact that our eating environments are constantly toying with us. When you suddenly realize that you've eaten half a dozen more chocolates than you should have, the reaction is never "Damn transparent bowl"; it's more often "Damn, I must have been hungry" or "God, why am I such a pig?"

Given this tendency to blame eating behavior on internal factors, like cravings or hunger, it's no wonder that those who eat a lot are demonized as gluttonous sinners, incapable of controlling their urges. No one attributes obesity to short glasses or transparent bowls; they attribute it to a lack of self-discipline.

None of this is to say that self-control and self-monitoring have no role to play in the regulation of food intake. The point, rather, is that the crude equation of obesity with gluttony (and the resulting moral condemnation of the overweight) is both counterproductive and simple-minded.

But enough about obesity; back to gluttony.

One of the real problems with mounting a defense of the "eating too much" mode of gluttony is that sinfulness is inherent in the concept. It's like asking whether murder is wrong. Murder is *defined* as unlawful killing. So yes, murder is wrong; it's a matter of semantics. What we should be asking is not whether eating *too much* is bad (it is by definition, given the negative judgment implied by "too much"), but whether eating *more* is worse than eating *less*.

The glutton's antithesis is the ascetic. It used to be that the ascetic was the solitary monk in a bare cell with a crust of bread and some water to sustain him as he sought communion with God. The modern incarnation of the ascetic is the dieter. The dieter's cell is more metaphorical than literal; instead of water and bread we find all manner of wheatgrass-like faddish things, and the communion sought, while still suspiciously spiritual, is less often with God than with the ideal image of oneself.

There is perceived virtue in dieting, not only because it brings health benefits, but precisely because it embodies the self-discipline and purity that overindulgence does not. And although moderation and restraint sometimes glow with virtue, at other times it's indulgence that has the halo.

Food for Thought

Take a few moments to try to solve the following problem:

> Below are two configurations of beads, mounted on
> pegs. Your task is to turn the configuration on the left
> into the configuration on the right, using as few moves
> as possible.[12]

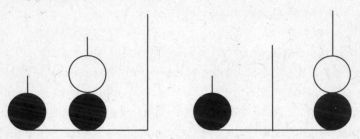

If you happen to be on a diet, you won't be very good at this. At least, not as good as someone who isn't watching his or her weight.[13]

This exercise is quite similar to what we psychologists call the Tower of London task. Such exercises are used to measure executive functioning, which is the mind's capacity to regulate and control thought and to make complex decisions. The mind's executive is much like a company's executive: It runs things, plans, and generally directs operations. And just as the executive of any large organization requires ample resources to successfully run the show, so too does the brain's managing director require cognitive resources to run the business of the mind.

So what's wrong with dieters' executives? Why can't those watching their weight deal very well with the Tower of London?

One possibility is that dieters are preoccupied with food-related thoughts. Such a preoccupation uses up limited cognitive resources.

So while the dieter's executive is off worrying about what to eat for dinner, it's unable to efficiently do other things.[14]

Another explanation is suggested by the work of University of Albany psychologist Matthew Gailliot.[15] For Gailliot, the crucial player in the executive functioning game is $C_6H_{12}O_6$, a simple monosaccharide. Its common name: glucose.

Glucose is the body's fuel. It's also the brain's fuel. Our bodies turn the food that we eat into glucose, which is carried in the bloodstream to the brain, where it powers our thinking.

One can view glucose as a resource, which is used up by effortful mental activity. And one kind of effortful activity is the constant self-control exerted by dieters in trying to regulate their eating. According to Gailliot, glucose used up in self-control tasks is glucose unavailable for other demanding cognitive activities.

Does this mean that dieters are condemned to suffer the consequences of chronically underperforming executives?

Not quite. It turns out that a well-timed glucose hit may actually protect us against the depleting effects of self-control.

In one clever study, Gailliot and a long list of collaborators brought participants into the lab and had them watch a short film.[16] The unusual thing about this film was that every ten seconds a word would flash in one of the bottom corners of the screen. Some participants were explicitly instructed not to look at these words. These participants were in the self-control condition because they had to consciously regulate their behavior, redirecting their attention back to the action of the film should their gaze happen to drift onto the words. Other participants were not given these instructions; they were told to watch the film normally.

After watching this movie, participants were given a drink and asked to rate it for pleasantness and other similar characteristics.

Unbeknownst to participants, however, some were drinking lemonade sweetened with sugar, while others were drinking lemonade sweetened with a sugar substitute. Both drinks tasted equally sweet; the difference was that the sugary drink provided a source of glucose, whereas the artificially sweetened drink did not.

What Gailliot was interested in was whether a glucose hit would protect those in the self-control condition against performance decrements on a subsequent task. Remember that according to the glucose-as-resource account, participants who exerted effortful self-control while watching the film should have depleted their glucose stores somewhat, which means less energy for subsequent demanding tasks. Would a simple drink of lemonade counteract this effect?

To answer this question, Gailliot next had participants do the following task. Try it yourself.

Name the colors that these words *are printed in*. Do not read the words, but name the colors.

Black

Gray

Black

White

Gray

This is called the Stroop task, and it is used by psychologists to measure selective attention, which is a central component of executive functioning. When people do this, and you probably noticed this yourself, they find it quite difficult to stop themselves from *reading* the words. For example, when the word "black" is printed in gray ink, it takes longer to say *gray* than when the color of the font and the word match. You can't help reading "black," and this slows you down.

What Gailliot found was that, as expected, participants who had previously engaged in self-control during the film were pretty bad at the Stroop task, *unless they drank the sugary drink*. These glucose-enriched participants performed just as well as those who didn't engage in any self-control during the film.

And it's not just executive functioning that gets a boost from a glucose hit. This miraculous monosaccharide has a range of interesting consequences for behavior. It helps regulate attention. It helps regulate emotions. More glucose means better memory, faster reaction times, less aggression . . . the list goes on. Glucose may even help us cope with death.[17]

So the glutton who nabs that last glass of soda may actually be a little smarter than the dieter, a little faster, and a little better equipped to face the great beyond. All positives to be sure, but can we go further? Is the glutton, so often the moral outcast, actually morally superior to the dieter?

The Good Food Guide

I want you to picture Barry. Barry is a "typical Australian man." Now I want you to imagine what a day in the life of Barry would be like.

If you're like many, this imagined day would be peppered with stereotypical assumptions: Barry might spend the morning riding around on a kangaroo, half drunk, shooting koalas, before returning home to his wife, Sheila, for an afternoon BBQ, some more beer, and an evening in front of the TV, watching cricket or *Neighbours*.

Most of us can bring stereotypes to mind with unsettling ease: the athletic African American; the hardworking Asian; the illiterate, surfer Australian; and the gin-soaked, bad-teethed Brit. The annoying thing is that stereotypes often come to mind without our intending them to. They are "automatically activated": by merely thinking about or encountering members of a stereotyped group, an interconnected web of group-related, stereotypical information comes to mind. One simply imagines "Barry," and one almost can't help thinking "kangaroo."

But *activation* is not the same as *expression*. A stereotype may present itself to *us* (that is, become activated), but we need not present it to *others:* We don't have to express the stereotypes that come to mind. We can in fact often suppress stereotypical information when it pops into our heads, pushing it back down into the brain's recesses, but this requires effort and cognitive resources.

Now, if one brings Gailliot's glucose logic to stereotyping, one could speculate that people with sufficient levels of glucose might be better able to engage in the effortful struggle to suppress stereotypes.

To test the possibility that glucose reduces stereotype expression, Matthew Gailliot and some colleagues showed people a picture of Sammy, a "typical gay man," and asked them to write a short story describing what Sammy might do during an average day.[18] The critical manipulation was this: Before writing their stories, half of Gailliot's participants were given a sugary drink (easily and quickly processed by the body into glucose), and half were given an artificially sweetened placebo, containing no calories, and thus offering no glucose boost. When Gailliot later coded participants' stories for stereotypical content, he found that people who had consumed the sugary drink were less likely to describe Sammy in a stereotypical fashion. These glucosed-up participants had the extra processing reserves required to suppress their stereotypes. They probably *thought* stereotypical thoughts while imagining Sammy's day, but they were able to refrain from expressing those thoughts in their stories.

So drink naturally sweetened lemonade and stereotype less. This is good news for the glutton, but just how far do the effects of consumption go in the realm of morality?

Barbara Briers, of the HEC School of Management in Paris, and her colleagues brought a group of people into their lab to do a couple of short studies on taste preferences and donation behavior.[19] The researchers had asked participants not to eat for the four hours prior to coming to the lab and to drink only water, tea, or coffee. This ensured that they were all reasonably hungry when they arrived.

When they got to the lab, half the subjects were assigned to the "satiated" group. These people did a taste test first, during which they ate what Briers calls simply "a big piece of cake" and then answered some questions about the cake's taste, color, texture, and so on. Then, after a twenty-minute interval, a donation task was administered, in which participants were asked whether they would be willing to donate to a bunch of different charities—the Red Cross, Doctors Without Borders, and so on.

The other half of the participants did exactly the same tasks, but in the reverse order—donation, then taste test.

The crucial difference between these groups was that those who did the donation task first were hungry while contemplating their donation preferences, whereas those who did it second were full.

What was of interest to Briers and her colleagues was the influence of hunger on subjects' willingness to donate.

Previous research has shown that certain aspects of food and money are processed in similar parts of the brain—the orbitofrontal cortex (OFC) to be precise, which sits just above the eye sockets.[20] The OFC is implicated in the processing of rewards. And what's interesting about the OFC is that it doesn't seem to matter what kind of reward we're talking about. Whatever it is—food, money, sex, drugs—if it involves rewards, it seems to involve the OFC.

The fact that food reward processing shares neural real estate with money processing suggested to Briers that money and food might, in some sense, be substitutable.

There is a Cree Indian saying: "Only when the last tree has died and the last river has been poisoned and the last fish has been caught will we realize that we cannot eat money."

Well, don't tell Briers or the OFC. As far as the orbitofrontal cortex is concerned, one can eat as much money as one wants. At the level of the brain, the desire for food looks much like the desire for money. So a hungry person might crave not only cake, but also cash. And just as the hungry person may hoard food, she may also have the urge to hoard whatever money she has.

This is exactly what Briers and her colleagues found: Hungry people were less likely to donate than those who had gobbled down a piece of cake.

Briers found a similar result when hunger was induced with the scent of baking brownies: Those who smelled baking brownies, and thus presumably felt hungry, gave less money to an interaction partner than did people not exposed to the scent.[21]

The upshot of this is that hunger may be less of a noble state than the ascetics would have us believe. Hunger is functional, not spiritual. It drives the organism to hoard—food, yes, but other rewards too.

In defending gluttony, one must address not only the charge of eating much versus eating little, but also the plethora of other complaints outlined by killjoy Middle Ages monastics hell-bent on stripping all pleasure from culinary experience. Remember Gregory's expansive list: too much, too greedily, too expensively . . .

The comprehensiveness of these prohibitions reflects the complexity of our relationship with food. For humans, food is much more than a simple energy source. Eating is not just a consumption experience; it is an aesthetic experience, a social experience, an identity-constituting experience. For early theologians, indulging any of these experiences too enthusiastically could distance oneself from God. But what of these other brands of gluttony for our everyday well-being? We have covered eating much versus little. What about the others? Let's begin with "too expensively."

The Cost of Gluttony

When it comes to eating, expectations matter: If a chocolate pudding has "healthy" on the label, people think it tastes better; if restaurant customers believe their wine comes from North Dakota rather than California, they think it tastes worse; given the choice between "chocolate cake" and "Belgian Black Forest Double Chocolate Cake," people will go for the second every time.[22] Expectations, be they health or taste based, change the experience of what we eat.

One of the strongest expectation generators when it comes to consumption is price. We know from research in marketing that as the price of a product goes up, so do perceptions of quality.[23] The same goes for food and drink.

But just how strong are price-based expectations? Can they change the very nature of our culinary experiences?

Picture before you five wineglasses, each filled with a different Cabernet Sauvignon. You're asked to taste these wines and rate them for pleasantness and intensity of taste. The five wines are differentiated by only their price tags.

Wine 1: $5
Wine 2: $10
Wine 3: $35
Wine 4: $45
Wine 5: $90

So, which wine do you prefer?

Well, when Hilke Plassmann of Caltech and some of her colleagues did exactly this study, she found, as might be expected, that people tended to like the higher-priced wines more than the lower-priced ones.[24] A closer look at Plassmann's data shows, for example, that wine from a $45 bottle was preferred to wine from a $5 bottle, and a $90 bottle was preferred over a $10 one. This makes sense: Price often reflects quality.

But, as is the case with many stories in social psychology, there is a twist here. You think you're tasting five different wines? Well, think again. You are in fact tasting only three: Wines 1 and 4 are exactly the same, as are wines 2 and 5. So although Plassmann's participants found the $45 wine significantly more pleasant than the $5 wine, they were in fact rating *the same wine*.

What's happening here is that expectations are driving experience. A $45 dollar wine *should* taste better than a $5 wine; a $90 bottle *should* be of a much higher standard than a $10 bottle. It is these "shoulds," rather than the basic physical properties of the wines themselves, that shape our pleasure experiences.

So the glutton who eats "too expensively" will indeed experience more pleasure. The interesting thing, however, is that simply *believing* that one is eating more extravagantly seems sufficient to do the trick.

The Spice and Bitterness of Life

When Pope Gregory hinted at the fact that we shouldn't be too concerned with how food is prepared, he was really trying to convince us that we should be content with the same boring grub, day in and day out. In essence, he was trying to bias us against variety.

Now, although folk wisdom has it that variety is the spice of life, when it comes to food, not all kinds of variety are equal.

Consider this scenario: You and a few friends sit down to dinner at a fancy restaurant. A waiter brings over some menus. You take a few minutes to peruse them and then you order.

At this, the ordering stage of the meal, variety presents itself in a few different guises. The menu itself is often an embarrassment of riches: duck risotto, penne ragu, eggplant parmigiana (this happens to be an Italian restaurant), caprese salad, primavera ravioli, lasagna . . . you get the idea.

The good news about variety on menus is that it often prompts healthier food choices. Because choosing from a long list is more difficult than choosing from a short one, people tend to make decisions that are easier to justify. And when seeking justification for their food choice, diners often favor health reasons over purely hedonic ones, such as taste. So when people in one study were given the choice of fruit or cookies, 55 percent chose fruit when there were only two options in each category. But when six fruits and six kinds of cookies were offered, a healthy 76 percent chose fruit.[25] More variety, healthier choices.

There is, however, an important caveat here: Offer too much variety and people seem to go into some kind of meltdown. Give people twenty-four kinds of jam to choose from and they're much less likely to make any choice at all than if they have to pick from only six jam varieties.[26] Such decision paralysis, or analysis paralysis as it's sometimes known, places a clear boundary on the value of variety. Offer enough to trigger mindful deliberation, but not so much that the mind shuts down.

Although menu option variety sometimes serves us well, the belief that variety *per se* is a good thing often proves detrimental.

Chances are that while you and your dining companions are glancing at your menus, something like the following conversation will take place:

> YOU: What do you think looks good?
> DINING COMPANION 1: The duck risotto looks pretty tasty.
> DINING COMPANION 2: Are you going to get the risotto? I was going to get that.
> YOU: Well, why don't you get the duck and I'll get the lasagna . . .

This sort of thing happens all the time—diners attempt to distribute variety around the table. Something seems not quite right about everyone ordering the same dish. This rests on the idea that variety is a good thing—the spice of the dinner table. But this kind of variety, the kind distributed across diners at the same table, often backfires.

Dan Ariely of Duke University ran a clever field study that explored the impact of such variety on food preferences.[27] (Beer preferences, actually, but let's not get pedantic.) With Jonathan Levav, a professor at Columbia, Ariely went undercover in a beer hall in Chapel Hill, North Carolina. Dressed as waiters, Ariely and Levav approached groups of customers and offered them free beer samples. Four samples were on offer: an amber ale, a lager, a pale ale, and a wheat ale. For some tables, customers were provided with these options and were then asked which beer they would like. Customers then proceeded to order, sequentially and out loud, around the table. For other tables, however, Ariely and Levav gave each customer a small menu and asked them to silently write down their preferred beer. After all the samples were served, customers were asked to rate how much they enjoyed their beverages.

What Ariely and Levav discovered should be heeded next time you're out dining with a group of friends: Customers who ordered out loud opted for more variety, but most people at the table *enjoyed their beers less* than those who ordered silently.

It's pretty clear what's going on here. Imagine it: You see the list of samples and you think, "The lager sounds pretty good, I'll get that." When ordering in silence, you simply write down this preference, and you get what you wanted. But when ordering out loud, your friend might order the lager before you, and so you decide, in the name of variety, to get something else instead. As a result, you end up drinking something that you didn't really want.

So the pursuit of variety distributed across diners may not be so sensible. But what about variety in one's own food choice? Well, again, it depends.

Let's go back to the Italian restaurant. Forget about your dining companions for the moment and focus just on what you want to order.

You're in the mood for an appetizer and an entrée and you notice that the restaurant does appetizer and main serving sizes of the duck risotto, which happens to be your favorite. Despite your inordinate love of gelatinous rice-based dishes, you probably wouldn't order risotto for both first and main courses. And this would be a sensible move. With each bite of a particular dish, our pleasure diminishes. This is called hedonic adaptation or habituation. The first mouthful of the risotto tastes great, the second very good; but by the time you get to the end of the course, each bite is delivering less and less pleasure and you're in the mood for a change. You've habituated.

So when consumption experiences follow close upon each other, like appetizer and entrée, variety seeking makes sense. Switching to a different dish for the main course, the parmigiana, for example, is a wise decision—even though it's not your favorite, it's still more pleasurable than more of the same old, adapted-to risotto.

But let's say we inject a sizable delay between first and main courses. In the spirit of an ultraslow food movement, you're invited to a restaurant for an appetizer one night and a main course a week later. You are asked to order both courses the first week—the appetizer for immediate consumption, the main for dining the following week. How would you order? Well, if you're like most, you would still opt for variety: risotto tonight and parmigiana next week.

But this isn't the optimal move.

Variety in consumption is useful when it wards off habituation. But with a long enough delay between consumption experiences, habituation is no longer a problem. The first bite of the main course of risotto *next* week will taste just as sweet (well, just as savory) as the first bite of the appetizer this week. Enough time has passed that habituation doesn't apply.

So when it comes to variety in food we need to be careful. The gluttonous gourmand who seeks a variety of culinary pleasures may be maximizing health benefits and pleasure in some circumstances, yet diminishing them in others. Variety in food, much like spice, should be used sparingly and wisely.

Ah . . . the French

In the end, understanding gluttony in the contemporary world really comes down to understanding the difference between the French and the Americans. In fact, it comes down to two crucial differences.

As hinted at earlier, French people have quite different attitudes toward food than do Americans. This difference is neatly illustrated by a couple of the questions that University of Pennsylvania psychologist Paul Rozin typically uses to measure food attitudes. Consider these:

1. Which word is most different from the other two?

BREAD   PASTA   SAUCE

2. "Fried egg" belongs best with:

BREAKFAST   CHOLESTEROL

If you're French, you're more likely to choose "bread" for the first question and "breakfast" for the second.[28] These choices betray a set of culinary associations linking food to the experiential and pleasurable aspects of eating. "Pasta" naturally goes with "sauce" (so "bread" stands out), as does "fried egg" with "breakfast."

Americans, on the other hand, are more likely to link "bread" with "pasta," drawing the carbohydrate connection, and "fried egg" with "cholesterol." These answers highlight the American pre-occupation with the nutritional aspects of eating. For Americans, culinary *experience* is much less important than culinary *consequences*. Americans are concerned with what food does to the shape and function of their bodies. To put it simply, in France, food is about pleasure; in the United States, it's about worry.

The other crucial difference between these countries is not attitudinal, but environmental. To appreciate the difference we can again turn to the work of Paul Rozin.

Rozin sent some members of his research team, equipped with portable digital scales, on a mission to weigh portion sizes in restaurants in Paris and Philadelphia.[29] These researchers would go into a local bistro or pizza joint, pull out their scales, and weigh a typical portion of food. When Rozin analyzed the results of this research, he found something quite startling: Across all the restaurants studied, American servings were about 25 percent larger. Even identical chain restaurants, which place a high value on standardization, differed between cities. Compare a McDonald's or Pizza Hut in Philadelphia with one in Paris, and you'll find the Philadelphian servings to be about 1.3 times larger. A large soda is not as large in Paris (530g) as it is in Philly (545g); a medium serving of French fries is 90g in the French capital, 155g in Philadelphia.

And it's not just in restaurants that you find these differences. Larger portions are built into every corner of the US food environment. Prepared foods from American supermarkets have portion sizes about 1.4 times larger than those in French supermarkets. Even American cookbooks tend to up the serving size by a factor of 0.25 over their French counterparts.[30]

Americans are living in the midst of an overwhelming abundance of convenient calories. They live in a supersized food environment. The French do not. And this makes all the difference when it comes to understanding gluttony in the modern world.

Here's the deal: In America the *attitude* is ascetic, geared toward restraint and nutrition, but the environment is not. The American culinary landscape is a vista of mountainous servings of easily obtained, calorie-dense food. So despite the attitudinal drive toward health in the United States, we observe the environment-driven spread of obesity. The French, on the other hand, approach food the way Pope Gregory's glutton would: with pleasure-seeking abandon. But the environment is structured so that these libertine tendencies are constrained. Once again, gluttony is not so simply a sin. Rather, it is a refreshing attitude toward food that can, in the wrong circumstances, lead us astray.

The equation of gluttony with obesity in the modern world has fostered a one-dimensional, puritan, and boring view of food and eating. All that matters for many of us is whether the next mouthful will make our butts bigger. The French, however, have remained steadfastly multidimensional in their culinary attitudes. For the French, eating is not just shoveling fuel into one's mouth; eating is not just eating.

For much of human history food has played an integral role in human societies—not simply as a consumption experience, but as an identity-constituting experience and a profoundly social one. Eating defines us. We are what we eat after all, both literally—proteins, water, glucose, etc.—and symbolically. Food speaks of where we come from (chow mein or tabouli), where we rank (foie gras vs. Big Mac), and what we value (vegetables or meat). Even regular old soup signals identity: chicken noodle soup = homebody; chili beef = the life of the party; New England clam chowder = the wit.[31]

Perhaps even more important, eating connects us with others. Food sharing is the forge of social bonds: It played a central role in the evolution of our species, binding males and females within households and cementing the larger community.[32] The evening meal, which has played so central a role in human households over evolutionary history, remains an important familial glue. There is evidence to suggest that families that eat together, thrive together, having better communication patterns and rearing children who perform well at school and have better psychological health.[33] Even the semantics of food and society are intertwined: The word "companion," for example, has its roots in the Latin "com" (together) + "pānis" (bread).[34]

The French have retained much of what is meaningful, pleasurable, and social about eating. They remain true gourmands, true gluttons in Pope Gregory's terms. They value experience, not consequence; sociality, not isolation; sensible variety, rather than plainness and monotony. And if this is what gluttony looks like, then I'd happily join the ranks of the French on their gluttonous descent into hell.

CHAPTER 3

Greed: Buying Happiness, Hard Work, and Self-Reliance

In Oliver Stone's classic 1987 film *Wall Street*, a slick-haired Michael Douglas addresses a boardroom of investors as the iconic Gordon Gekko:

> The point is, ladies and gentlemen, that greed, for want of a better word, is good. Greed is right. Greed works. Greed clarifies, cuts through, and captures the essence of the evolutionary spirit.[1]

Gekko embodies that particular brand of 1980s morality that placed faith in the ultimate goodness of the free market. The individual's pursuit of self-interest (read: the individual's greed) would guarantee the welfare of the masses, save the day, and so on. We (consumers) didn't have to do much but spend, and the market would take care of the rest. Few of us believed the extreme version of this after 1987; fewer still after what Wikipedia dubs the "Financial Crisis of 2007–2010."

Clearly the "greed is good" claim doesn't quite capture the

complexity of things. But neither does the equally trite "greed is bad." This simplistic view has it that the recent global economic downturn, and others like it, was a symptom of the unbridled greed of the marketplace. But things are never that simple. Market crashes have all manner of causes: political infighting, decision-making biases, the specifics of market regulation, the group psychology of shareholders . . . the list could go on. What's more, money and our pursuit of it is a constant; if one wants to blame greed for financial bust, then one must be willing to praise it in equal measure for financial boom.

But this chapter is not about greed in the marketplace. It's about greed in other aspects of our everyday life. And just as the role of greed in the market is a complex one, so it is in our everyday behavior.

The word "greed" derives from the Middle English "gredi," a word closer in meaning to modern English's "gluttony" than "greed." However, it is not the culinary that greed these days describes, but the monetary. Greed is a vice of money, and it is money that is at the heart of greed's contemporary status as a sin (or at least a pretty bad thing). In perhaps the most famous painting of the seven deadly sins, Hieronymus Bosch's *The Seven Deadly Sins and the Four Last Things*, greed is personified as a bribe-taking judge, accepting payment with one hand while condemning a petitioner with the other. In choosing cash over justice, the judge succumbs to money's all-powerful corrupting influence. The matter is put most simply by St. Paul: "Love of money is the root of all evil." The point is clear: Money is dirty and those who greedily pursue it are bound to muddy both their hands and their souls.

This chapter will challenge this received wisdom. And at the outset, let me just say that, far from being the root or indeed any organ of evil, money isn't half as sinister as you or St. Paul might think.

Happiness for Sale

One of the only things we enjoy more than damning the rich is pitying them. Those of us accustomed to the unpleasant sensation of the bottom of our pockets want to believe that the rich are pitiable souls, misguidedly chasing dollar after useless dollar on the path to inevitable depression and emptiness. It is commonly said that money doesn't buy happiness, and the financially challenged among us hope that this is true. But are we right?

The simple fact is that the more money people have, the happier they are. Rich countries are happier than poor countries and, within the borders of any one nation, the haves are happier than the have-nots. What's more, the effects of money on our well-being are varied. The rich are more satisfied with their lives, they have more positive experiences, they feel more enjoyment, and they experience less boredom, depression, and sadness than the poor.[2] In a recent and rigorous review of the literature, two young economists, Betsey Stevenson and Justin Wolfers, concluded:

> Income is positively related to wanting to have more days like yesterday, with feeling well rested, with feeling treated with respect, with being able to choose how to spend one's time, with smiling or laughing, with feeling proud, with having done something interesting, and with eating good-tasting food.[3]

Varied they may be, but the benefits of higher income are by no means guaranteed. The greedy can have all the money they want and still not get it quite right. In fact, when it comes to the purchase of happiness, it's very much a case of buyer beware. In spending your money on the good life, it's important to know what to buy.

A few years ago, Lexus ran an ad campaign with the following slogan: "Whoever said money can't buy happiness isn't spending it right."

This is a little smug coming from a luxury car company, but there is some truth in it.

As with much of psychology, philosophers got there first. So it is with the question of how to shop for happiness. Aristotle noted that although "men fancy that external goods are the cause of happiness" it is "leisure of itself [which] gives pleasure and happiness and enjoyment in life."[4] In this observation, Aristotle hits on one of the most important distinctions on the supermarket shelves: experiences versus material goods. Let's rephrase Aristotle slightly for the modern consumer: Is it better to do or to have?

With this question in mind, social psychologists Leaf Van Boven of the University of Colorado and Thomas Gilovich of Cornell University asked a group of college students to recall a purchase they had made "with the intention of advancing [their] happiness and enjoyment in life."[5] More specifically, they asked half of these students to recall an "experiential" purchase—a purchase of more than $100 that involved "spending money with the primary intention of acquiring a life experience—an event or series of events that you personally encounter or live through." They asked the other half about a "material" purchase—a purchase of more than $100 that involved "spending money with the primary intention of acquiring a material possession—a tangible object that you obtain and keep in your possession." As you would expect of college students, travel, dining out, and admission fees to concerts and ski slopes ranked highly among the experiential buys; clothes, jewelry, computers, TVs, and stereos were among the material.

The students then answered some questions about their purchases: How much did the purchase contribute to happiness? Was it money well spent? Proving Aristotle right (and not for the first time), experiential purchases made people happier than material ones and were thought to be better financial investments. The pleasures of the restaurant and the ski slopes outweighed those of clothes, jewelry, and TVs.

Now, college students aren't the most representative bunch. Does this pattern of results hold more generally? To answer this, Van Boven and Gilovich conducted a large-scale survey of over 1,200 Americans.[6] Over half (57 percent) said that buying an *experience* made them happier than buying a material possession; only 34 percent of respondents said the opposite (the remaining 9 percent weren't sure or declined to answer).

So what's so special about experiences? Why does dining out make us happier than buying clothes? For Van Boven and Gilovich, experiential purchases trump material purchases for a number of reasons.

Experiences, more so than material possessions, are important defining features of who we are. Material goods do define us, of course—think about what your clothes or CD collection say about you. It's just that experiences do it better. This question should illustrate the point:

If your house caught fire, what is the one possession you would save?

Most people say they'd save their photo albums—the document of their life experiences.[7]

Another reason that experiences bring happiness is that they are often shared—they involve other people. Dining out or going to the theater or to the movies are all activities we enjoy with others. And because other people play such a large role in our happiness, shared experiences contribute substantially to our well-being.

Finally, experiences age well. Unlike material possessions, whose unchanging physical realities are quickly adapted to, experiences, once lived, exist as memories, open to reinvention and reinterpretation. We may tire of material possessions, but we can constantly reinterpret the memories of our experiences through our proverbial rose-colored glasses. For example, when supporters of George W. Bush were asked how happy they had felt on the day when Bush was elected in 2000, they remembered (four months after the fact) feeling much happier than they actually had been.[8]

So the greedy pursuit of money can pay off if we know how to spend the cash we acquire. Money can indeed buy happiness, but we must exercise caution. We must remember that with more money often comes more stress and more responsibility.[9] And no matter how much of it you have, if you don't have people to share it with, money won't do you much good.[10] In fact, psychologists are beginning to understand that when it comes to happiness, the purchasing power of the dollar may pale against other, less tangible currencies. According to psychologists Ed Diener of the University of Illinois and Martin Seligman of the University of Pennsylvania, social relationships, enjoyment at work, and health are big contributors to happiness.[11] Money helps, but it's not all there is to it.

Nevertheless, the general rule holds: As income goes up, so does happiness. With quiet confidence in this relationship, we can next ask one final and important question: How much is enough? Is there an income beyond which I don't get as much "happiness bang" for my buck? The jury is still out on this point. Some research shows that once people hit a middle-class income, additional money doesn't make them that much happier; but other work shows sizable happiness increments all the way up to yearly incomes of $200,000 and above.[12]

All in all, the greedy among us are on the right track when it comes to happiness. But there are no guarantees. And just as we should be aware of money's limits in buying the good life, so should we appreciate that money does more than simply buy us things. According to Diener, money makes us happy in many other ways: The act of making money itself can be enjoyable, as can the act of spending it.[13] But money grants another important blessing: It's a powerful motivator.

The Money Motive

When I was a kid, I'd play pickup basketball at the schoolyard court across the street from my house. I wasn't particularly tall or fast or, for that matter, particularly good. I'd make the occasional basket and the occasional assist. But one Saturday afternoon, I remember, it seemed that I could do no wrong on the court. I was fouled early on and made both free throws. From then on, I made every shot I attempted. Disappointingly, this was a one-time experience. The following week I went back to being regular old average on the court. But for that one Saturday I had entered "the zone."

Be it during the weekend pickup game, the World Series, or

the Super Bowl, it's the goal of every sportsperson to enter that
semimystical state. When one enters the zone, all things are said
to move in slow motion, all perception becomes finely tuned, and,
most important, one scores a hell of a lot of points or goals or
touchdowns or whatever.

The zone—or the "hot hand phenomenon," as it is sometimes called—has not escaped the attention of social psychologists. The bad news for athletes, however, is that this elusive state
may not exist. In a classic study, psychologists Thomas Gilovich,
Robert Vallone, and Amos Tversky reviewed the shooting stats
of the Philadelphia 76ers and the Boston Celtics, looking for evidence of hot hands.[14] From the point of view of a statistician, a
basketball player has a hot hand if he is more likely to make a
basket after one or more successful shots than after one or more
misses. In other words, the key characteristic of the hot hand is
its "streakiness"—the stringing together of consecutive baskets.
Despite long and careful analysis of a mountain of stats, Gilovich
and his colleagues found no evidence of the hot hand phenomenon on the basketball court.

Now, NBA players are paid a hell of a lot, but they're not
really rewarded for putting in streaky performances. They're expected to make baskets, but not necessarily to make back-to-back,
consecutive strings of baskets. But what if players were paid
for *streakiness*? Could the promise of money actually create hot
hands?

Economists Todd McFall, Charles Knoeber, and Walter Thurman wanted to know whether the introduction of monetary incentives for streaky performance would create hot hands (hot clubs
perhaps?) on the golf course.[15] To do this, they made use of a for-

tuitous event in the history of the Professional Golfers' Association (PGA) Tour.

The prestigious PGA Tour consists of about forty-five tournaments played over the course of a year. Players who do well in each tournament get paid; those who do poorly don't. For a long time there was no real incentive for performing well in back-to-back tournaments. Of course, the better a player's performance in any one tournament, the more money he'd get, but there was no real incentive for racking up a streak. However, in 1987, the Tour Championship (originally called the Nabisco Championship) was introduced. Entry into this lucrative end-of-season tournament depends on players' performance throughout the tour, and only the top thirty money earners at season's end gain entry.

How did McFall and his colleagues make use of this fact in examining the effects of money on the hot hand? Here's how.

They reasoned that, before any particular tournament during the season, a player falls into one of the three groups.

Group 1: Those who already have a spot in the Tour
        Championship
Group 2: Those who have some chance of getting a spot
Group 3: Those who have pretty much no hope of a spot in
        the Tour Championship

Next, they reasoned that as the season progresses, the composition and size of each of these groups changes. At the beginning of the season, most players are in group 2, with some chance of making the championship, but as the season progresses more and more players move into groups 1 and 3. Toward the end of the season, with just a few tournaments left, there are relatively few players in group 2, as most have already either guaranteed themselves a spot in the championship (group 1) or have no chance of making the cut (group 3).

Finally, McFall reasoned that players' motivation for streaky performance would depend on both the group they're in and the time left until the end of season. And it's this last insight that allowed McFall and his colleagues to test whether the promise of money created hot hands.

Here's the thinking: Players at the top of the money list toward the beginning of the season have an extra incentive for streaky performance because they can secure their spot in the Tour Championship with a run of strong, back-to-back early performances. With this done, they can then ease off a little toward the end of the season. These players have the incentive to put in *early*-season streaky performance. However, those who find themselves in group 2 near season's *end* have an extra incentive for streaky end-of-season performance, as they try desperately to make the championship cutoff.

With this logic in mind, McFall compared the top-ranked to the thirtieth-ranked player at different stages during the season, while controlling for various nuisance factors such as player ability, course difficulty, and so forth. He predicted that toward the beginning of the season the top-ranked player would outperform the thirtieth-ranked player because of the increased motivation for early-season streakiness. And this is exactly what he found. The list leader performed about 0.13 strokes better than the thirtieth-ranked player. (Remember that player ability was taken into account, so this difference is not due to the top-ranked player simply being a better golfer.)

What should happen toward the end of the season? Well, at season's end, the thirtieth-ranked player is vying for a spot in the Tour Championship and should be trying extra hard to make the cut; the top-ranked player is guaranteed a spot, so can ease off. So the streakiness trend should reverse. And this is what happened. With just one tournament left before the championship, the thirtieth-ranked player performed about 0.56 strokes better than the top-ranked player (adjusted for ability and other factors). Importantly, this difference in performance as a function of time of season and money-list rank exists only after the 1987 introduction of the Tour Championship. Before this incentive was introduced, there was no hot hand in golf.

Two Paradoxes of Payment

The logic of the general rule is straightforward—if you want people to work harder and perform better, make the most of their greed and pay them. This is common sense and it is, on balance, empirically supported. It holds on the golf course, and it holds in the lab and the workplace—more money means harder work and better outcomes.[16] But as with all rules, there are important exceptions. If you look closely enough, you will come across two very interesting paradoxes of payment that you should be wary of if you're to make the most of greed as a motivational force.

Paradox 1: Extrinsic up, intrinsic down

Some years ago, psychologist Edward L. Deci of the University of Rochester conducted an experiment that was to become one of the classics of social psychology.[17] He was interested in the influence of money (and reward, more generally) on motivation. Deci built his study around an important distinction between two motivational types: intrinsic and extrinsic. Intrinsic motivation comes from love of a task itself. One plays the piano, for example, with intrinsic motivation if it is the playing of the piano *per se* that is the motivating factor. Extrinsic motivation, on the other hand, comes from outside. Money is a good example of an extrinsic motivator. Our pianist has extrinsic motivation if she plays for monetary reward. Deci was interested in the relationship between extrinsic and intrinsic motivation. What would money do to one's intrinsic motivational drive? Would tempting our pianist's greedy nature with money for her performance increase her intrinsic motivation or for some reason quash it?

With such a question in mind, Deci invited people to participate in a laboratory study. This study involved taking part in three testing sessions, each on a different day. On the first day, participants arrived at the lab and found before them an experimenter, a selection of puzzle pieces, and some magazines (including—don't you just love the '70s?—*Playboy*). Participants were told that they had thirteen minutes to build four shapes out of the puzzle pieces. A picture of each shape to be built was presented to participants on a piece of paper.

Now, at a certain point during the session, the experimenter left the room for eight minutes and observed participants through a one-way mirror. What Deci was interested in was how much of this "unsupervised" time each participant would spend on the puzzle. He reasoned that those with high intrinsic motivation (or puzzle love) would spend the majority of their time on the puzzle and less time reading *Playboy*.

The second session looked much the same as the first, at

least for some. For half the participants, the second session was an exact reconstruction of the first—experimenter, puzzle, *Playboy*. For the other half, however, a financial incentive for performance was introduced. These people were told that they would receive $1 for each shape that they built. As you would expect, those paid for their performance spent more unsupervised time on the puzzle (just over five minutes) than they had during the first, unpaid session (about four minutes). Those who weren't paid spent about three and a half minutes on the puzzle in each of their two sessions.

So far, the story is much the same as it was on the golf course: Paying people for performance increases their motivation. But what happens when you take that payment away? In the third session, each participant performed the puzzle task again, but this time under the conditions of session 1; that is, no one was offered any money. So did being paid in session 2 increase or decrease participants' intrinsic motivation during session 3? It actually *decreased* it. Those who had been previously paid spent considerably *less* time on the puzzle task in session 3 (just three minutes and twenty seconds). Those who hadn't been paid once again spent about four minutes on the task. So although the lure of cash during session 2 increased motivation, when this extrinsic motivation was taken away, it took participants' intrinsic motivation with it.

The reason is simple enough. If one sees oneself solving puzzles *for money* then one comes to think that the *only* reason for solving puzzles is money. Take the money away and one removes the only source of motivation. Money steps in and buys off intrinsic motivation. The lesson here of course is that if you start paying for performance, you had better keep paying.

Paradox 2: There are some things money can't buy
Take a look at these two lists of transactions:

List A	*List B*
Paying someone to clean your house	Paying your mother for cooking dinner
Buying food	Buying your way out of military service
Buying a house	Buying votes in an election

You probably have no problem with the exchanges on list A. It's perfectly reasonable to pay someone to clean your house and to exchange money for goods such as food or accommodation. But something might strike you as a little off about list B. If you're like most, you believe that while cleaning services, food, and houses can be bought and sold, motherly love, national service, and democracy cannot. And although the Beatles got it right when they sang "money can't buy me love," they don't seem to have gone far enough. Money also can't buy (or at least in most people's minds *shouldn't* buy) honor, trust, or election outcomes. While some goods and services are subject to the rules of the market and are open to pricing, others are not.

Psychologist Philip Tetlock of the University of California at Berkeley calls the list B transactions "taboo trade-offs" and has shown that most people react to such exchanges with moral outrage; the mere mention of trading duty for dollars and many folks fly way off the handle.[18] Money simply doesn't belong in the list B transactions. Family relations, national service, and voting are domains of life governed by social and moral norms, not the norms of the market.

To understand why money is acceptable in some exchanges and not others, we need to appreciate that people think differently about different kinds of transactions.[19] Some exchanges readily fit the market mold. In such situations, goods and services are traded for cash, and not a head turns. Your boss pays you for the hours you work, you pay the supermarket cashier for your groceries, and life goes merrily on. In these kinds of market exchanges, you weigh costs and benefits, attach prices to commodities, and generally let your inner economist have the run of things.

Other transactions (let's call them "social transactions") don't fit the money market mold at all, and introducing market principles into such exchanges just won't do. Paying mom for cooking a Sunday roast is not how things work, just as trying to buy votes and patriotic duty are deemed unethical. In such transactions, reciprocity and duty, not dollars and cents, are the appropriate currency.

Now, moral outrage is well and good when it comes to hypotheticals. We sit astride our high horses and rage at anyone who dares trade social goods for money, but how do we ourselves behave in such situations? Although the thought of others doing good deeds to satisfy their greed might make you indignant, what if someone offered you cash for helping an old lady across the street? Would you be more or less likely to do it? When it comes to actual behavior, do we remain atop our noble steeds or do we dismount? Can greed be co-opted in service of the common good? To answer this question, let's consider a very clever field experiment.

Every year in Israel there are a number of days on which schoolchildren go door to door soliciting donations for charity. They get nothing for this good work except the pleasant feeling that comes from doing a good deed. How would these well-intentioned kids behave if they were paid cash for their charitable efforts?

Economists Uri Gneezy and Aldo Rustichini were interested in just this question when they designed a field study to test the effects of payment on charitable behavior.[20] They took one hundred and eighty Israeli school students and assigned them to different groups. One group did their door knocking under conditions typical of volunteer work: They were reminded of the importance of the cause and that society wished them well. These students were offered no monetary incentive for their efforts. Another group, after hearing the same speech about the cause and the gratitude of society, was offered payment of 1 percent of the donations they collected. (Importantly, students were told that their payment would come out of the experimenters' pockets, not from the collected donations.)

So how much did each group collect?

If a real monetary incentive for a good deed rubs people the wrong way as much as does the hypothetical case, we'd expect that donation collectors who were paid would perform worse than volunteers. In Gneezy and Rustichini's study the unpaid volunteer group collected $68. (Donations were collected in new Israeli shekels, but I've done the currency conversion for you.) And those offered payment? Only $44—a substantial $24 less than the volunteers.

These results suggest that being paid for charity work may, in fact, backfire. Just as people recoil at the notion of *others* doing good deeds for cash, so too do they underperform if they themselves are offered payment. This finding suggests that greed can't be capitalized on to promote charitable works.

But consider an alternative explanation for the results. Perhaps payment backfired because the sum offered simply wasn't large enough. Perhaps the offer of a meager 1 percent led to worse performance because it was perceived as insultingly small.

To test this possibility we need to consider the third group in Gneezy and Rustichini's study. This group was offered payment of *10 percent* of the amount collected, rather than a paltry 1 percent. Now, if people are simply rejecting the notion of being paid *per se*, we'd expect this group to also collect less than the no-payment group.

How much did the 10 percent group collect? Actually, they collected almost as much as those offered no money at all—$63.

So when money is introduced into social transactions it may do more harm than good, but it depends on the sum. If the offer is too small, money may sabotage our good intentions. But if large enough, it doesn't seem to do much harm. The moral of the story: if you want to make the most of greed in the promotion of good deeds, you'd better pay enough or not pay at all.

With Money in Mind

Money need not be dangled before us, carrot-style, in order to influence our actions. Even the very *concept* of money, if activated somewhere in our minds, may be enough to change our thinking and behavior in quite astonishing ways. No one knows this better than social psychologist Kathleen Vohs. In a series of clever studies, Vohs has demonstrated just how powerful a grasp money has on our behavior.

By now you should realize that we social psychologists are a tricky bunch. When poor, unwitting participants come into a psychology lab, nothing is ever quite as it seems. Take one of Vohs's first experiments on the power of money.[21] When participants came into her lab, they were given a list of jumbled-up sentences. Some participants got a list that looked something like this:

> *flip coin now silver the*
> *the wealthy is man bench*
> *sky the seamless red is*
> *intense the latch heat is*
> *prepare the gift wrap neatly*
> *some he cash red wants*

Others got a list that looked more like this:

> *in the into park it's*
> *he'll course master the red*
> *somewhat prepared I was retired*
> *deep around the ditch past*
> *red past wise the benches*
> *athlete he bottle is an*

Regardless of the list they got, all participants had the same task: Form meaningful, four-word sentences out of each set of words.

Do you notice anything different about these two lists? In the first list, half of the items contain "money" words (cash, coin, wealthy). In the second list, none of the items contains money-related words. (In the actual study, each list contained thirty jumbled sentences, but hopefully you get the gist.) The point of this simple exercise is to very subtly prime participants with the concept of "money." Unscrambling money-related sentences gets money-related thoughts ready (or primed) for action.

After unscrambling the word sets, participants were given an "insight problem." When people do such problems they typically don't have a sense that they are making progress—rather, the solution comes to them in a lightbulb moment, in a flash of insight. Here's a classic example (the solution is in the notes):

Connect all nine dots by drawing four straight lines without lifting your pen from the page and without retracing the lines.[22]

The insight problem that Vohs used was chosen carefully so that people wouldn't be able to solve it too quickly. What Vohs was interested in was how long people would persist at the task before asking for help. Would those people subtly primed with "money" be more or less likely to ask for help in solving the task? After about only four minutes, the task had most people in the control condition (those who unscrambled sentences without money words) bewildered, and almost 75 percent had asked for help. People in the money-priming condition, however, were a lot more persistent—only after eight minutes had 75 percent of these participants sought help with the task.

Why? Vohs argues that money priming makes people *self-sufficient*, which for Vohs involves "an emphasis on behaviors of one's own choosing accomplished without active involvement from others."[23] In such a mind-set, people aren't likely to ask for help, preferring to rely instead on their own abilities.

Just how far-ranging are the consequences of money priming and the money mind-set? To test the boundaries of this money-induced self-sufficiency effect, Vohs's team brought another willing group of subjects into the lab. These participants were given either a stack of cash or a stack of cash-shaped pieces of paper to count. Each person counted out his or her stack as an ostensible finger-dexterity task. It should come as no surprise by now that this was just a cover story. The counting task was simply a way of priming "money" for some of the participants (those counting cash). After this, the experimenters rather unceremoniously plunged participants' hands into a bucket of hot water. The money-primed felt less pain![24]

This is more compelling stuff: The mere idea of money makes us resistant to pain? Just as physical riches help make the wealthy more self-reliant, so too does the *idea* of money allow us to feel invulnerable, capable.

Does what goes for physical pain also go for social pain? In another of Vohs's studies, she once again used the cash-counting manipulation to prime "money," but this time, instead of plunging participants' hands into hot water, she had them perform a social interaction task in which they were socially excluded.[25] Once again, the money-primed participants were better off: They felt less hurt after being ostracized than those who counted paper. The money mind-set served as a buffer, this time against the social pain of ostracism.

It is in this last finding that the greedy, money mind-set reveals its two faces. In placing confidence in the self, one tends to feel less need for others. Such self-reliance may have varied and positive consequences, as discussed earlier, but it may also have negative consequences.

Greedy individuals who chronically have "money on the brain" are often condemned as being selfish and heartless. There might seem something to this view at first glance.

One of the mental shifts that accompanies the money mind-set is a reduction in what we psychologists call perspective taking. This is simply the ability to put oneself in other people's shoes and see the world through their eyes. We have various ways of measuring it. Here's one of the most interesting—try it:

> With the index finger of your dominant hand (the one
> you write with) trace the letter "S" on your forehead.

That's all there is to it. How does this simple exercise measure our ability to see the world through another's eyes? It's all in the direction of the "S" that you drew. If you began your "S" at the top right of your forehead and moved your finger to the left, then you drew an "S" as it would look from your own perspective. In other words, you didn't put yourself in the shoes of another. If, however, you began your "S" at the top left and traced your finger to the right, then you did put yourself in another's shoes—the "S" you drew is the right way around for someone looking at your forehead.

In another of Vohs's studies, some participants performed this exact task.[26] Other participants did something slightly different. They were asked to draw a "$" on their foreheads. The $ version of the task is *physically* very similar, but *conceptually* very different to the plain S task—it primes the concept of money. What did Vohs find when she had participants do these tasks? Those who drew the dollar sign were less likely to put themselves in the shoes of another than those who did the task with a regular old "S."

If money-primed people are less likely to see the world through the eyes of others, are they also less likely to help others? In another clever experiment, Vohs and her colleagues looked at whether priming people with money influenced their helping behavior.[27] This time, when participants arrived at the lab they found the board game Monopoly laid out on a table before them. Subjects played Monopoly for a short time with a stooge in Vohs's employ and then the critical manipulation was made.

After a while, the experimenter cleared away the board to make room for the next task. However, while for some participants the game was cleared away entirely, for others, the experimenter "inadvertently" left $4,000 of Monopoly money on the table. To further boost this money prime, the $4,000 group was asked to imagine a future filled with abundant finances. The other participants, the controls, were asked to think about their plans for the next day.

Having firmly activated "money" in the minds of some, it was time to test their helping behavior. To do this, Vohs staged an accident. She had another confederate walk across the lab carrying a folder and a box of pencils. When the confederate reached the participant, she spilled the pencils all over the floor. The experimenters were interested in how many pencils the participants would pick up. What they found was that money-primed participants picked up significantly *fewer* pencils than those in the control condition.

This all looks like rather bad news for the chronically money-primed greedy. But although this lack of help may be thought selfishness by some, it is important to consider these results together with Vohs's other findings. A closer look suggests that it is not selfishness that accounts for what's happening here. A selfish person would try to maximize her benefits at all costs. But remember the first of Vohs's studies: Money-primed people waited *longer* than control participants before asking for help on a difficult task. The selfish participant would presumably have asked for help almost immediately in order to solve the problem as quickly as possible.

According to Vohs, the money mind-set is not intrinsically selfish, but rather *self-sufficient*. In fact, far from being imbued with an immoral selfishness, this mind-set may have its own kind of morality built into it. In addition to making people self-sufficient, money priming also emphasizes market exchange principles. Thinking about money leads people to focus on aspects of the marketplace, like transaction and exchange, costs and benefits, inputs and outputs, and so on. As Vohs argues, because of their focus on market rules, money-primed people may prefer exchange relationships (in which they receive something for any helpful act they perform) that are regulated by the highly democratic (and not at all immoral) norm of equity.

Our relationship with money is complex. On the one hand, it can make us happier, more motivated, and self-sufficient—all consequences that count in favor of the greedy pursuit of the dollar. On the other hand, it has the potential to sabotage our motives and make us less helpful. And if we value money too much, become too materialistic, and forget about friends and family, we can get trapped in a maze of destructive choices.

The complexity of this relationship springs partly from the

fact that money acts on our minds in two basic ways. According to
psychologists Stephen Lea and Paul Webley of the University of
Exeter, money can be seen both as a tool and as a drug.[28]

If we see money as a tool, a mere instrument of exchange or
an incentive, things tend to go quite well. Tools are simply in-
struments we use to achieve more valued ends. Just as a hammer
is useful in building a table, so too is money helpful in achieving
happiness, performance, and self-sufficiency.

But money also has powerful addictive properties—it can take
hold of us like a drug. When this happens, money is no longer a
means to an end, no longer a tool we use to gain some reward, but
the end itself. When greed becomes an addiction, we're in trouble.
As soon as we start to sacrifice our friends, family, and other aspirations to the pursuit of cash, things start to go wrong.

CHAPTER 4

Sloth: Slow, Lazy, and Asleep Wins the Race

The *Oxford English Dictionary* lists several definitions for "sloth."[1] This is one:

An edentate arboreal mammal of a sluggish nature, inhabiting tropical parts of Central and South America.

This is another:

As a "proper term," by later writers taken to mean: A company of bears (or erroneously, boars).

These aren't sins, of course, unless your god happens to be offended by grossly out-of-proportion, tree-dwelling mammals and/or the improper use of collective nouns.

It's actually *OED* definition 1a that we want:

Physical or mental inactivity; disinclination to action, exertion, or labor; sluggishness, idleness, indolence, laziness.

But this isn't really a sin either. It reads more like a Sunday afternoon. Or a Saturday for that matter. Or even the occasional workday.

So just why is sloth a sin? Well—and here we can spread the blame around a bit—it's due partly to the noonday laziness of Middle Ages monks and partly to the semantic sloppiness of the church, but mostly to the Protestants.

Originally, it wasn't "sloth" that was on the list of deadly sins, but "acedia," which is Latin for a kind of spiritual laziness, malaise, or despair, a rather more sinister disposition than the *OED*'s benign "disinclination to action." It's unclear to me precisely what a lazy spirit is, but it was something that Middle Ages monastics were apparently a little uneasy about. Presumably, despairing spirits resided in slack, sluggish bodies, the hands of which were destined for all manner of devil's work. Evagrius Ponticus, the monk who first listed the deadly vices, writes that sloth would compel the monk to "look constantly towards the windows, to jump out of the cell, to watch the sun to see how far it is from the ninth hour, to look this way and that."[2]

All this jumping about sounds rather unslothlike to me, but the point is that monks were expected to contribute to the physical and spiritual well-being of their communities, and any spiritual malaise that had them looking this way and that and jumping out of their cells would likely undermine such commitment. Religious leaders didn't want their followers walking off into the godless desert after the midday meal, abandoning faith and fellow monks. So they institutionalized acedia as a mortal sin.

That was then. Over time the church itself seems to have gotten a little lazy with the semantics of sloth. The insidious "acedia" was replaced with the innocuous "sloth," and as a result, we have a contemporary injunction against the rather benign state of "taking it easy."

Now, only part of sloth's current bad reputation is the direct legacy of its deadly status. As I mentioned, this is mostly the fault of the Protestants. With the Protestant Reformation of the sixteenth century came the equation of work with salvation, an equation that the great German sociologist Max Weber dubbed the "Protestant work ethic."[3]

With this notion of work as redemption comes the idea of sloth as an economic sin. Any taking it easy that occurs is less likely to be seen as an offense against God than as an offense against the economy. It is not the health of the sinner's soul that contemporary antisloth moralists worry about, but the health of the bottom line. The noontime malaise of the modern sloth manifests only rarely as a soul-searching sojourn into the desert. Instead we have Facebook poking, Twitter tweeting, and MySpace whatever-ing, all of which might be bad for business, but hardly bad for the spirit.

Work undoubtedly provides meaning and means for us all, but the blind adoration of the Protestant work ethic is troubling. Bertrand Russell, for one, wasn't happy about it: "The notion that the desirable activities are those that bring a profit has made everything topsy-turvy," he writes in *In Praise of Idleness*.[4] The problem with the work = virtue belief is the invalid corollary: sloth = vice. For when one pits virtuous work against sinful sloth, the sin becomes synonymous with inactivity, with doing nothing.

But this opposition misses a crucial point. In truth, sloth actually constitutes a lot of activity, it's just that much of this activity is unseen unless looked for. Robert Louis Stevenson captures it in his *Apology for Idlers*: "Idleness so called . . . does not consist in doing nothing, but in doing a great deal not recognized."[5] The goal of this chapter is to convince you of this. And we see Stevenson's point no more clearly than in that ultimate of slothful states: sleep.

Sleep on It

For all its seeming simplicity, sleep remains something of a mystery to scientists. From the outside it looks about as complicated as a brick: eyes closed, the occasional murmur, maybe a toss here and a turn there. This general lack of apparent function might give the impression that the brain shuts down during sleep, so that it, like us, can get some rest. But this is not the case. The sleeping brain is the ultimate Stevensonian—it does a hell of a lot that is not recognized by the casual observer.

Scientists have known about the consequences of sleep, and lack of it, for quite some time. Sleep debt has been related to increased risk of heart disease, susceptibility to the common cold, and risk of diabetes.[6] Most of the really interesting research on the benefits of sleep, however, comes not from the medical domain, but from the psychological.

Robert Stickgold of the Harvard Medical School has spent a considerable part of his career researching sleep. One of the key insights from the past few decades of his research is that the brain does a lot of work shaping our memories while we're asleep. The sleeping brain works hard to consolidate the information we have been processing during the day. According to Stickgold, sleep sews together the fabric of our memories, strengthening associations and forging new connections.[7] And it does so in a rather creative and useful way.

Consider the following list of words and try to remember them.

Nurse
Sick
Medicine
Health
Hospital
Dentist
Physician
Ill
Patient
Office
Stethoscope

Now turn the page and answer the questions that follow.

Was "sick" on the list? What about "doctor"? How about "nurse"?

Answers: yes, no, and yes. Interestingly, when people do this task they are quite likely to mistakenly "remember" that the word "doctor" was on the list.[8] (Look back, it isn't.)

This little demonstration highlights an important property of human memory. What happens in this task is that the brain encodes the *gist* of the word list and tends to forget the details. From words like "ill," "stethoscope," and "hospital," the brain picks up the obvious medical theme, and then when tested, it uses this theme to make an informed judgment about what was likely to have been on the list.

Our brain is quite good at gist processing when we're awake. But it turns out that it may be even better at it when we're asleep. With Jessica Payne of Harvard and numerous other colleagues, Stickgold gave participants a task like the preceding one at 9 P.M. one evening and then tested them at 9 A.M. the following morning, after a night's sleep. Other participants were presented with word lists at 9 A.M. and then tested in the evening, after twelve hours of being awake. What Stickgold and Payne found was that gist processing was significantly more pronounced after sleep than after the same amount of time spent awake. Sleepers were more likely to recall the word "doctor," even though it wasn't on the list.[9]

Although this result suggests that sleep leads to *worse* memory performance—"recalling" words that weren't there—this apparent maladaptiveness is actually quite useful for everyday functioning. We are bombarded with so much detailed, often redundant information during the course of our lives that we seldom need to remember all the ins and outs. Extracting the summary meaning or gist from a set of stimuli is often much more efficient than laboriously retaining and processing all the details.

Other forms of memory are also well served by sleep. Emotional memories and other types of declarative memory (i.e., memory for facts and events, or "what" memories) are also solidified by a good night's sleep.[10] And procedural memory, too —the term we use to describe our memories of *how* to do things—also gets a boost.[11]

But it's not just memory that gets a kick start from sleeping. One of the real benefits of the sleeping brain's creative needlework is seen in a study by Ullrich Wagner of the University of Lubeck.[12]

Wagner gave participants a series of puzzles, consisting of patterns of three digits. For example:

$$1 \quad 1 \quad 4 \quad 4 \quad 9 \quad 4 \quad 9 \quad 4 \ldots$$

$$\underline{\quad} \quad \underline{\quad} \quad \underline{\quad} \quad \underline{\quad} \quad \underline{\quad} \quad \underline{\quad} \quad \underline{\quad} \ldots$$

Participants had to produce a second line of digits by using the following two rules:

1. If two consecutive digits are the same, respond with that digit.
2. If two consecutive digits are different, respond with the third digit.

Beginning on the left, the first two digits are 1 and 1, so—applying rule 1—the response is 1, and a 1 is written in the first space on the second line. This response, 1, and the next number, 4, are different, so applying rule 2, the next response is the other digit, 9. And so on.

Below is the completed sequence.

1	1	4	4	9	4	9	4...
	_1_	_9_	_1_	_4_	_4_	_1_	_9_ ...

This kind of problem might seem tedious (and it is), but there's a shortcut. And if you can see the shortcut, you can solve the problem much more quickly. Can you see it? (Hint: look for a pattern in the second line of numbers.)

What you may have noticed is that there is a mirror image in the second to seventh digits in the second line (the last three digits—4, 1, 9—are a mirror of the second to fifth digits—9, 1, 4). If you notice this pattern, then you can complete such puzzles without using the rules.

This is another insight problem for which the solution simply pops into consciousness in an "aha" or "lightbulb" moment.

Wagner gave participants in his study some practice with these sorts of puzzles and then tested them on similar puzzles eight hours later. Some were trained in the morning and came back to be tested in the evening; others were trained in the evening and came back the next morning after having slept through the night. So what does sleep do to insight?

Of those who stayed awake between training and testing, 23 percent discovered the shortcut. This percentage more than doubled for those who slept: 59 percent of the sleepers managed to see the trick in the puzzle.

Why does this happen? Again, it's because of the way the sleeping brain processes and structures information. Not only do our dozing brains synthesize memories to extract the gist, they also restructure our memories and mental associations into interesting and novel patterns. And it is this creative reweaving of our associative networks that leads to that "aha" moment.

Now, it would be annoying if we required a full eight hours every time we wanted a little insight. Thankfully, the benefits of sleep aren't restricted to our night-long somnambulatory efforts. Naps work, too.

UC San Diego psychologist Sara Mednick is a nap expert. And in research done with Denise Cai and other colleagues, she tested the influence of naps on creative problem solving.[13]

In one of her studies, Mednick gave participants a Remote Associates Test (RAT). This is a kind of word-association exercise that requires you to think of a word that ties together a group of three other words. Here's an example:

cracker, union, rabbit

Can you think of a word that links these three? (The answer: jack.)

Along with the RAT, Mednick gave participants a series of analogy puzzles involving questions like these:

Chips are to salty as candy is to _____.

The answer: "sweet."

Mednick gave participants these puzzles at 9 A.M. and then had them return to the lab at 1 P.M. When they returned, she had some people take a ninety-minute nap and asked others to simply rest quietly in a chair and listen to music. Then, later in the day, Mednick had participants come back to the lab and do another RAT.

What she found was that nappers who had experienced REM
sleep (rapid eye movement sleep, the stage that often involves viv-
idly recalled dreams) solved about 40 percent more RAT puzzles
in the second session that they did before their nap. Non-nappers
showed no such improvement. And, importantly, nappers who did
not experience REM sleep during their nap showed no performance enhancement either.

There's a further twist here. An important point to note is that
some of the RAT puzzles that participants were tested on later in
the day had the same solutions as the analogy puzzles that participants completed in the 9 A.M. session. For example, the answer
to the RAT problem "cookies, sixteen, heart" is "sweet," which
matches the solution to the analogy puzzle noted previously. And
it's only for these RAT problems, those whose solutions were also
solutions to the morning's analogy puzzles, that REM sleep con-
ferred an advantage. When participants were tested on the same
RATs as they were trained on or on completely novel RATs, sleep
did nothing to performance.

What this suggests is that REM sleep is not simply improving memory in general, but more specifically influencing the way
that previously encountered information (e.g., answers to the
analogy puzzles) is integrated into the mind's associative networks. What the REM brain does is spread activation out across
our associative networks from the concepts and ideas that we
have encountered during the day. We are primed with the word
"sweet" in an analogy puzzle, for example, and then when we
sleep, the brain sends out ripples of activation to associated
concepts, such as "heart," "sixteen," and "cookie." Then, when
we are later given the RAT problem "heart, sixteen, cookie,"
we can more easily come up with the answer because our REM

brains have already strengthened the appropriate connections to "sweet."

Of all sleep-related phenomena, dreams have perhaps the most resounding resonance with everyday life. We don't directly experience gist memory forming nor do we feel activation rippling out across our minds' networks, but we do experience and remember our dreams.

So what are dreams exactly? And what are they for? These are tricky questions, but recent work suggests that dreams may be an experiential window into what the brain is doing while we're asleep.[14] I said that we don't have direct experience of memory formation and spreading activation. That's true. But we might have *second-hand* experience. Dreams may actually provide a consciously accessible reflection of the brain processes occurring during sleep.

Erin Wamsley of the Harvard Medical School and her colleagues were interested in the effects of sleep on basic maze-navigation abilities.[15] So she brought participants into her lab and trained them on a virtual, 3-D navigation task. After training, half the participants were allowed to nap for ninety minutes, while the other half were kept awake but in a resting state. Later in the day, all participants were tested on the same maze to see how quickly they could navigate it.

Again we see the benefits of napping: Those who napped got through the maze faster than those who stayed awake.

But that's not the interesting part. Wamsley also woke people during their naps and asked them what they were dreaming about. Most reported not dreaming about the maze, but those who did showed a tenfold improvement over those who didn't.

Now, it's unlikely that dreams somehow *cause* task improvements. It's more likely that they *reflect* the brain processes that lead to performance enhancement. Dreams play out, in images and other sensory phenomena, the processes of gist formation, procedural and declarative memory consolidation, and creative insight that the brain engages in during sleep.

There are still numerous mysteries about how the sleeping brain works, not the least of which concern dreaming. But even this preliminary survey should convince you that this most slothful of states does a lot for us, much of which is very useful.

Daydream Conceiver

Do you remember what the previous paragraph was about? It's OK, I'm not offended. Chances are that your mind will wander for up to eight minutes for every hour that you spend reading this book. About 13 percent of the time that people spend reading is spent not reading, but daydreaming or mind-wandering.[16]

But reading, by comparison to other things we do, isn't so badly affected by daydreaming. Some estimates put the average amount of time spent daydreaming at 30 to 40 percent.[17]

It's fine to dream while you're asleep; you can't help it. But doing it while you're awake seems to speak of some mental deficiency, a lack of discipline or character, or at the very least a lack of attentiveness. For antisloth moralists, defenders of disciplined productivity above all else, what mind-wandering amounts to is no less than a deadly sin.

And they have a point—but only up to a point. The wandering mind is by definition less engaged in the task at hand (reading this book, for example), and this disengagement can lead to poorer task-related performance (e.g., recalling the content of a previous paragraph). But when the mind wanders, it often meanders down avenues more interesting and more important than the one you're currently on.

When we daydream, our attention becomes decoupled from the current environment and turns inward to our feelings and thoughts. But the wandering mind doesn't simply stroll down any old mental path; it heads toward thoughts and feelings that are of some significance to us: our future plans, our everyday problems, our memories. So while we're reading *War and Peace*, or indeed this book, we may catch ourselves in a moment of reverie about a loved one or an upcoming exam or some important client at work.

Although dwelling on such issues may seem a rather obsessive, ruminative tendency, our minds' constant preoccupation with the things that are important to us may in fact be helpful.

In one study, psychologists Deborah Greenwald of Northeastern University and David Harder of Tufts found that the content of people's daydreams reflected the kinds of coping strategies that they typically employed to solve problems.[18] This suggests that the wandering mind might actually be off searching for ways to cope with the stresses of everyday life. You may not know exactly how to deal with your man troubles, but your wandering mind is working on it.

Daily troubles aren't the only problems that mind-wandering might help us solve. Allowing the mind to amble in slothful bliss may actually improve performance on other kinds of tasks as well.

One of the most interesting things about this slothful pastime is that it involves the same brain regions that are active when people are solving insight puzzles. These kinds of puzzles, remember, involve finding a solution that simply pops into one's head. Although "aha" moments might appear to come out of thin air, a distinctive pattern of neural activity precedes them. In the time leading up to the successful solution of an insight problem, there is increased activation in a variety of neural areas, including the posterior cingulate cortex, the anterior cingulate cortex, and the middle and superior temporal gyri.[19] The particulars of these brain regions don't really matter for our purposes. The important point to note is that these areas, among others, are also activated during mind-wandering.

What's even more interesting is that mind-wandering might actually be the brain's natural state. When the mind wanders, parts of the brain that make up the so-called default network are activated. This network is a complex of brain areas that are typically active when we are resting. (Again, the particulars don't matter, but for those who are interested, the prominent default network areas include the medial prefrontal cortex, the posterior cingulate cortex/precuneus region, and the temporoparietal junction.[20]) This collection of brain regions is the default because it is active when the brain is not occupied with external processing demands. It's thought to reflect the processing of internal information, thoughts, and memories—those things that are continually important to us and are often the foci of the wandering mind. This overlap between mind-wandering and the default state of the brain has led researchers to speculate that "mind-wandering constitutes a psychological baseline from which people depart when attention is required elsewhere and to which they return when tasks no longer require conscious supervision."[21]

The wandering mind may be a creative genius, but it is an absentminded genius. We may be off dreaming up creative solutions to our love troubles while reading *War and Peace*, but our

memory for who's related to whom in Tolstoy's complex genea-
logical matrix will suffer. Sometimes we need to focus, even if the
task at hand is dead boring. So here's a remedy for the wandering
mind.

Jackie Andrade of the School of Psychology at the University of Plymouth in England asked perhaps not one of the most
important scientific questions of the twenty-first century, but certainly one pertinent to our project here: Can doodling possibly
counteract mind-wandering's drawbacks?[22] The study design was
straightforward:

1. Get people to listen to a boring audio recording that's
   likely to induce mind-wandering: "Hi! Are you doing
   anything on Saturday? I'm having a birthday party and
   was hoping you could come. It's not actually my birthday,
   it's my sister Jane's. She'll be twenty-one . . . I've also
   invited her boyfriend William and one of her old school
   friends, Claire . . . I can't believe it has got so cold
   already . . . Jenny from next door is going to bring a quiche
   and I'll do some garlic bread . . " You get the picture.
2. Give half of the participants instructions to doodle during
   the task (give the other half no such instructions).
3. Spring a memory test on participants after the recording,
   asking for recall of names and places mentioned in the
   recording.

Now, we know that mind-wandering can hamper memory
performance on such tests. Does doodling offer some protection
against this? The results of Andrade's study: doodlers recalled 29
percent more information than nondoodlers did.

Precisely why doodling offers this protection is not quite clear, but for now here's a free yet sage piece of advice: When you're sitting through your next long, slow, mind-numbing Monday morning meeting (or while you're reading the rest of this book), doodle.

Lazy Heads

By some accounts, if you want to be an expert at anything, you need to devote about ten thousand hours to it. This is unwelcome news to the sloth. The ten-thousand-hour rule (which can be translated into the ten-year rule, calculated at about 2.7 hours per day) seems to apply to becoming a chess grand master, a world-class violinist, or a Beatle.[23]

This is clearly unacceptable. The sloth doesn't want to spend ten thousand hours doing much of anything. But take heart. It's not always a case of more is better. When it comes to making complex decisions, the lazy mind of the sloth, the mind that eschews the sweat-inducing effort of conscious thought, may actually be better off.

Psychologists have known for quite a while that a lot of our thinking happens without much effort at all. Experiments show that we can and do form impressions and make judgments after very little time. What's more, these offhand, effortlessly formed impressions are often just as accurate as more arduously formed ones.

Take a study by Nicholas Rule and Nalini Ambady from Tufts University.[24] They showed people a series of photographs of male faces. The key manipulation was the presentation time of the photos: Some participants could view the photos at their own pace; others saw each photo for a rather lengthy 10 or 6.5 seconds; and yet others saw the photos for just 100, 50, or 33 milliseconds.

The participants' task was to judge whether the man in each photo was gay or straight. The pictures had been selected from online personal ads, so the researchers knew the sexual orientation of the men photographed and thus had a standard against which to judge participants' accuracy. The results showed that participants in all time conditions except 33 milliseconds (possibly because 33-ms presentations may be outside of subjective awareness) categorized the photos above chance levels. Importantly, participants' accuracy was just as good in the 50-millisecond condition as it was when they had 10 seconds to look at the photos. Having plenty of time to scrutinize and theorize brought no benefits.

Bringing no benefits is one thing. It also happens that the effortful, scrutinizing conscious mind can actually leave us worse off.

In one study by Timothy Wilson and Jonathan Schooler, both at the University of Virginia at the time, participants were brought into the lab to do a taste test.[25] When they arrived, they found before them five jams—and not just any jams. Wilson and Schooler had chosen them specifically to represent a range of quality. They chose the five strawberry jams that a group of experts had ranked 1st, 11th, 24th, 32nd, and 44th on a long list based on sweetness and aroma and a bunch of other jam-relevant attributes.

Participants were asked to taste each jam and then rate their liking for each one. However, not everyone did this in the same way. Half of the participants were instructed to analyze why they felt the way they did about each jam before making their evaluations. These people engaged in conscious deliberation about the reasons why they liked or disliked each jam. After tasting the jams, they were given a questionnaire on which they listed their reasons. The other half of the participants were given a different questionnaire after the taste test, asking them to list reasons why they chose their university major. After completing these questionnaires, all participants then rated how much they liked each jam.

If effortful deliberation and the close analysis of reasons improves decision making, we would expect there to be greater agreement between the participants who reasoned about the jams and the jam experts. Wilson and Schooler found exactly the opposite: The preferences of those participants who had thought about their college majors lined up better with the experts' opinions. Those who thought consciously about why they liked the jams ended up making "suboptimal" preference ratings.

The reason for this difference is that the conscious mind is subject to decision biases that the lazy, unconscious, or distracted mind (the one thinking about college majors) avoids. When we consciously deliberate about a choice, we tend to put undue weight on attributes that are accessible, plausible, and easy to verbalize.[26] And doing this can lead to preferences and decisions that are less than perfect. Just because we can verbalize a thought about, say, the packaging or price of a strawberry jam doesn't mean that packaging or price are relevant factors in determining our preferences.

The real problem with conscious thought comes down to the fact that the conscious mind is limited in its capacity to process information. Our stream of consciousness is only so wide, a mere trickle in comparison to the surging river of the unconscious. According to unconscious-thought theory, proposed by Ap Dijksterhuis, professor of psychology at Radboud University in the Netherlands, during unconscious thought information is processed, organized, and weighted in a more optimal fashion than during conscious thought.[27]

So what exactly is unconscious thought? The official definition: "object-relevant or task-relevant cognitive or affective thought processes that occur while conscious attention is directed elsewhere."[28] This is precisely what was happening for those participants in Wilson and Schooler's study who were thinking about college majors. Although they knew they would later have to make preference ratings about the jams, their conscious minds were temporarily engaged in another task, allowing their unconscious minds to process jam-related information in a manner free from the biases of conscious thought.

There are, of course, limits to this theory. If the processing constraints of conscious thought can be overcome, then effortful, conscious thought and unconscious thought are about equally good in guiding decisions and choices.[29] Nevertheless, there is mounting evidence that effort-free, slothful, unconscious thought can often lead to better judgments about most anything, from jam to university courses, from artwork to apartments.[30]

Slothful Saints

Jam and cars, paintings and apartments. The effects of unconscious thought on judgments about these things are interesting, but hardly worthy, you might argue, of raising slothful thinking to the status of virtue. Well, how about this: Unconscious thought may actually make us more moral.

Jaap Ham, Kees van den Bos, and Evert Van Doorn, all at Utrecht University at the time, presented people with information about four job application procedures.[31] One description was of a fair procedure, one was of an unfair procedure, and the other two were of procedures of somewhat middling fairness.

After reading all the information, participants were asked to rank the procedures in order of most to least just. However, not all participants did so immediately. The key manipulation, as in most studies of unconscious thought, was what people did between reading and judging. Some were asked to give their justice judgments immediately, others were asked to consciously deliberate on the fairness of these procedures for about three minutes, and yet others were told that they'd be asked for justice judgments, but not yet—first, they'd be required to do another task. These participants, in the unconscious-thought condition, did a distracter task, the two-back task (in which they were presented with an ongoing stream of single-digit numbers on a computer screen and asked whether or not the current number matched the number presented two positions previous). They did this for three minutes and then made their justice judgments.

With judgments about morality, you might think that conscious thought should be a better guide than unconscious thought. We may waver on which jam, car, or painting we like, but surely we can apply moral rules and principles in a deliberative and conscious fashion to judge right from wrong. If so, you would expect that participants who had time to consciously deliberate about the fairness of job procedures would be most accurate in their justice judgments.

What Ham and his colleagues found was that justice accuracy scores were higher in the unconscious-thought condition than in the immediate and conscious-thought conditions (these latter two conditions didn't differ in accuracy). To the authors, this hinted at a kind of unconscious morality that outperforms both deliberative moral reasoning and rapid moral intuition.

Again, the reason may lie in the way that information is weighted in the conscious versus the unconscious mind. Justice judgments are often complex and involve lots of information that needs to be appropriately integrated in the formation of a judgment. Immediate judgments don't give us enough time to adequately weight all the relevant information, and conscious judgments involve biased weighting schemes. As in judgments of jams and cars and paintings, the lazy, unconscious mind weights morally relevant information appropriately, relatively free of bias, and so leads to more accurate judgments.

The Idea of Slow

Gray, wrinkled, bingo, Florida.

If you were now to get up from your chair and walk to your kitchen, you would do so more slowly having read these words than if you hadn't read them. "Gray," "wrinkled," "bingo," and "Florida" are all part of the stereotype of elderly people. Any other stereotypical terms come to mind? "Blue rinse," "knitting"?

When John Bargh, a social psychologist at New York University at the time of this study, and his colleagues Mark Chen and Lara Burrows presented participants with these words and others, embedded in scrambled sentences, something quite remarkable happened.[82] After unscrambling the sentences containing elderly stereotype words, participants were told that the study was over and that they could leave. In fact, the study wasn't quite over yet. The experimenters surreptitiously timed participants as they walked from the experiment room to a nearby elevator. In one of the most fascinating findings in the past couple of decades of social psychology research, Bargh found that participants exposed to the elderly stereotype took significantly longer to reach the elevator than did those in a control condition, who unscrambled sentences containing neutral words.

This effect is another example of priming. When people are

exposed to words like "Florida" and "wrinkled," activation spreads from these to other, related concepts that are linked because they are part of the elderly stereotype.

What happened in Bargh's study was that exposure to the elderly stereotype primed the concept "slow," and this activation leaked out into behavior, slowing participants down.

So just thinking about slowness, and not even intentionally, can impact the way we act. Walking down a hallway is innocuous enough, but the concept of slow, when primed, can have quite beneficial consequences.

In a study applying Bargh's work to driving, Rob Gray and Russell Branaghan of Arizona State University primed participants with the elderly stereotype and then put them in a driving simulator.[33] What Gray and Branaghan noticed was that drivers were more cautious when operating under the elderly stereotype prime than when under no prime. (They also found that the teenage stereotype, primed with words like "sophomore" and "date," sped drivers up.)

The most startling thing about this research is that these primes work unconsciously. Participants aren't aware that the concept of "slow" has been primed, yet it nevertheless exerts a considerable force on people's behavior, bringing out their inner sloths and, in this case, making them better drivers.

Slow and Steady

In 1999, four Italian towns signed a pledge to take it all a bit easier, to slow down and smell the roses, or whatever floral delights happened to grace the Italian countryside. This pledge initiated a movement, Cittaslow ("Slow Cities"), which has since, somewhat ironically if not self-defeatingly, picked up considerable momentum. More and more, cities and towns around the world are opting to slow down, embracing many of the Cittaslow manifesto's fifty-five pledges. From cutting traffic and noise to expanding pedestrian and green zones, towns from Katoomba in Australia to Ludlow in England and Sonoma in the United States have all worked hard to ease the pace of life and earn the coveted Cittaslow certification.

Of course, some places are already slower than others and don't really need to hear Cittaslow activists preaching the virtues of sloth. California State University psychologist Robert Levine and his students have spent a considerable amount of time studying the pace of life around the world. Over the years Levine has collected data from cities in more than thirty countries and has been able to rank them from fastest to slowest.[34] Of course, measuring a country's speed is no straightforward task, but Levine eventually settled on three indicators: walking speed (the speed at which pedestrians cover sixty feet); work speed (the speed at which postal clerks complete the sale of a stamp); and the accuracy of public clocks (a benchmark meant to assess a country's overall concern with time).

So which country is the fastest overall? It's Switzerland. Not surprisingly, they rank number one on clock accuracy. They are also up there on the other measures. Then come Ireland, Germany, and Japan, with Italy ranked fifth (Cittaslow was sensible to start its mission at home). This top five grouping is consistent with Levine's other work, which suggests that people tend to move faster in large, industrialized cities with vibrant economies and cool climates.[35] At the bottom of the list we have the more slothful, slower countries: Syria, El Salvador, Brazil, Indonesia, and, slowest of all, Mexico.

Some countries may be more sloth-prone than others, but does it matter? Implicit in slow movements of all kinds, from Slow Cities to Slow Sex and Slow Schooling, is the notion that easing the pace of life is a good thing—that slowing down will bring more happiness and health and myriad other blessings. Well, is it true? Are slow cities somehow better off than fast ones? It appears so.

When Levine turned his attention from different countries to different cities within the United States, he found that inhabitants of American cities with faster walking, talking, and working speeds were at higher risk of developing coronary heart disease.[36]

But it's other work by Levine that provides one of the clearest insights into the virtues of sloth. In 2008, with Stephen Reysen and Ellen Ganz, both also at California State University at the time, Levine asked: does the pace of life in cities have any effect on helping behavior?[37] Here's what these researchers did to answer this question.

First, they measured the pace of life in twenty-four US cities. These cities were sampled from the stereotypically torpid South (e.g., Louisville, Nashville, Dallas), through the West and Midwest, and up to the frenetic Northeast (e.g., New York, Boston). In each of these cities, the researchers measured pedestrian walking speed across sixty feet as an indication of pace of life. (Just for the record, New York doesn't top the list of fastest US cities. It ranks seventh, with people taking an average of 13.10 seconds to cover sixty feet. San Francisco is the fastest at 12.44 seconds.)[38]

Next, they measured helping behavior in these cities using three different yet equally clever techniques:

1. The dropped pen. The experimenter, while walking toward a subject, "accidentally" dropped his pen in the subject's

full view. A second experimenter, following twenty to thirty feet behind, recorded whether the subject displayed helping behavior. The subject was deemed to have helped if she picked up and returned the pen or called out to the first experimenter, telling him that he'd dropped it.

2. The hurt leg. Here the experimenter, decked out in a leg brace and limping heavily along the sidewalk, approached a subject and "accidentally" dropped a pile of magazines. Again, if the subject offered to help or actually assisted the ostensibly injured man in retrieving his magazines, she was deemed to have helped.

3. Change for a quarter. The experimenter walked straight up to a subject, quarter in hand, and asked politely for change. If subjects checked their pockets for coins, they were deemed to have helped.

So does walking speed influence any of these helping behaviors? It certainly does. Whether it's picking up pens or magazines, or searching for change, people in slower cities do more of it.

Granted, this study comes with all the interpretational ambiguity of any correlational design. It leaves open the question of causality. We can't tell whether walking slowly somehow causes more helping, whether helpful people tend to dawdle, or whether some third variable leads people both to slow down and to help.

To clarify the causal connection, we need an experiment. Thankfully, we have one in the shape of an elegantly designed classic of social psychology, a study that has come to be known as the "Good Samaritan" study.[39]

We were reminded of the Good Samaritan parable in the lust chapter. For those who have forgotten:

A guy gets beaten up and pretty much left for dead on the road from Jerusalem to Jericho. As he lies on the roadside, he is passed by a priest and a Levite (who was also a religious functionary), who fail to offer any help. But a passing Samaritan stops and helps, bandaging the man's wounds and taking him to an inn.

The obvious moral of this story—that religious belief doesn't, in and of itself, make one a good person—occurred to John Darley and Daniel Batson, both psychologists at Princeton at the time, but so too did something a little less obvious. They reasoned that because Samaritans occupied a rather low rung on the social ladder, they may have been operating on a more relaxed time schedule than the high-ranking priests and Levites. In their words: "One can imagine the priest and Levite, prominent public figures, hurrying along with little black books full of meetings and appointments, glancing furtively at their sundials. In contrast, the Samaritan would likely have far fewer and less important people counting on him to be at a particular place at a particular time, and therefore might be expected to be in less of a hurry than the prominent priest or Levite."[40] In other words, it seems as though Samaritans had their own Cittaslow movement going on.

This is an interesting thought, but how to be certain? Like all good psychologists, Darley and Batson decided to test the idea, and to do so, they recreated the Good Samaritan parable on the Princeton campus. Here's how.

They recruited seminary students to take part in a study, ostensibly on religious education. In a first testing session they measured aspects of these students' religious convictions: Is religion, for you, a quest for meaning? Is it a means to an end? And so on. In a second session, the experimenters staged the parable. Students reported to this second session and were told that they'd have to deliver a short talk, three to five minutes long. For half the students, the talk was to be about jobs to which seminary students would be suited; for the other half, the talk was to concern the parable of the Good Samaritan, a copy of which was provided.

Next came the key manipulation.

Students were told that the building they were in was a little short on space and that they'd have to report to another building, just next door, across an alley, to give their talks. One third was told to hurry: They were late and they should dash across as fast as they could. Another third was told that they were expected any minute. These participants were, in the words of the experimenters, in an "intermediate-hurry." And the final third was given the impression that they had all the time in the world.

Out in the alley, participants came across a man slumped in the doorway, a man that Darley and Batson were determined should look "somewhat ambiguous—ill-dressed, possibly in need of help, but also possibly drunk or even potentially dangerous."[41]

So just how Samaritan-like were these students? Did they help? Overall, only 40 percent of these students (seminary students, don't forget) offered some form of help. But of more interest to us is the difference in helping between the hurry conditions. Of those students who were told that they were late and to hurry, only 10 percent offered any help. Of those with plenty of time, a more encouraging 63 percent helped the victim. (The intermediate hurriers were intermediately helpful: 45 percent helped.)

Slowing down brings out the altruist in us. But why? It's unlikely that sluggishness, through some witchery, reweaves our moral fiber or reveals some previously unthought-of moral truth, transforming us into unusually caring, selfless human beings. Rather, easing the pace, releasing the inner sloth, and getting our heads out of our own concerns allow us to attend a little more closely to the needs of others.

By slowing down, we overcome what social psychologist Stanley Milgram termed "psychological overload."[42] In modern, industrialized societies, especially in the large cities in these societies, we are bombarded with sensory information of all kinds. In an effort to cope, we block out what isn't relevant to our current goals. So it's not that fast movers are less moral, it's just that they have blinders on to anything that could potentially distract them from their current purpose.[43]

The Cittaslow manifesto is rather hefty at fifty-five pledges. Still, the work covered in this chapter suggests that we could bulk out the manifesto just a little. We could add more sleeping, napping, and daydreaming; less effortful, conscious thought; and walking a bit more slowly. As with the other sins, sloth does have its drawbacks. Indulge it too often and you'll never get anything done. But indulge it appropriately and you'll be smarter and perhaps even a little more virtuous for your (lack of) effort.

CHAPTER 5

Anger: The Positive
Negative Emotion

When I was a kid, about five years old, I hit a girl. I think her name was Suzie, and she may have been Chinese. I can't really remember. But what I do remember is that she was being annoying, and so I hit her. I'm not sure whether I knew that I wasn't, as a boy, meant to hit a girl. But it was an instinctive reaction. There was nothing I could do. My arm was a physical extension of the annoyance and frustration and anger that I felt. The reaction was natural, simple, and driven completely by her irritating, taunting voice. At least that's how I tend to justify it to myself. I felt angry and so I lashed out.

Anecdotes like these, with their implication that anger = violence, is the stuff that gives this sin its bad name. You would, of course, be excused for thinking that anger and violence are the same thing. In historical depictions of the sin, the link is tightly and quite literally drawn. Medieval images representing anger (or *ira*, as it was known then, from the Latin) typically portray sword-wielding maniacs. And in Bosch's painting *The Seven Deadly Sins and the Four Last Things*, again the angry man carries a sword (although here he seems to be attacking a monk with a table on his head; I'm not sure of the significance of that). In contemporary culture too, anger and violence are one: In David Fincher's *Se7en*, anger is murder.

But they are not the same, anger and violence. For one, they're not the same on definitional grounds. Violence is, technically, the exercise of physical force so as to inflict injury on, or cause damage to, persons or property. At least that's what the *Oxford English Dictionary* says.[1] Anger is something else.

For psychologists, anger is, first, an emotion. When we psychologists talk about emotions we have in mind a complex blend of the physiological (heart rates and hormone levels), the experiential (subjective feelings and sensations), the behavioral (fight or flight tendencies), and the cognitive (beliefs and mind-sets). Anger has its own constellation of these components. It is accompanied by the sensation of the pulse quickening, a general tension of the body, and a narrowing of focus.[2] There is also an actual elevation of heart rate, muscular changes (more frowning and less smiling), and rising blood pressure.[3] None of this entails violence in any way.

One might be tempted to argue that although not technically synonyms, anger and violence may still be quite closely associated. Anger may routinely *cause* violence, for example. Well, it may, some of the time, but it doesn't do so very often. In fact, one estimate suggests that violence follows anger in only about 10 percent of cases; another estimate puts it as low as 2 percent.[4] Anger is neither a necessary nor a sufficient cause of violent behavior.

So at the outset, put violence from your mind. I am not talking here about hitting or kicking or killing. I'm talking about that feeling you get when you are cut off by an inconsiderate driver or when your child keeps on and on about wanting another cookie before dinner. For our purposes, it's important to realize that one can experience anger without feeling the need to kill the driver, your child, Kevin Spacey, or indeed anyone else.

Approaching Anger

With violence removed, anger starts to look less menacing. Sure, there's still the gritted teeth and furrowed brow, but don't let this fool you. At its heart, anger actually looks more like a positive emotion than a negative one.

Many psychologists still group anger among the negative emotions. Like fear, sadness, and contempt, people believe there's something untoward about anger. This is mostly because it is often triggered by unpleasant events. There are, understandably, some drawbacks to the emotion: The anger-prone are more likely to have a heart attack and other cardiovascular problems, and are also at greater risk of anxiety, alcohol abuse, and unsafe driving behavior.[5]

But despite these minor annoyances, anger researchers are beginning to ask whether this emotion is a negative one at all.

Consider the following study by Mario Mikulincer of Bar-Ilan University in Israel.[6] Participants come into the lab and are presented with a series of puzzles. These involve discovering the rule underlying a series of patterns. They do this for a while, but no one seems to do very well. Actually, not a single participant can uncover the hidden rule. This is not surprising, given that Mikulincer used unsolvable problems in this study. There was, in fact, no rule to discover. He did this because he was interested not in performance, but in people's reactions to failure.

Participants began the task with a goal in mind: Discover the rule. But all were prevented from reaching their goal. How did participants respond? Some expressed dejection and sadness at their failure, feeling depressed that they didn't succeed. Others, however, got angry. When Mikulincer then gave his participants a second task, this time a task with a solution, those who felt anger performed better. They persisted longer at this second task, and their persistence paid off.

Mikulincer's study highlights two points central to understanding the benefits of this sin. First, it hints at the fact that anger is often triggered when our goals are blocked. It's anger we feel when the vending machine takes the last of our change or teases us by at first gesturing toward dispensing a Mars bar, but deciding at the last minute to keep it.

The second thing Mikulincer's study highlights is that anger is a *motivator*, a drive to keep trying, to persist. It's this sin that keeps us rocking that vending machine back and forth until it releases its stubborn grip and lets the Mars bar fall with a satisfying clunk into the dispenser tray. (That or—and here's another downside to the emotion—the vending machine falls on top of us, seriously injuring or killing us, as it does to numerous people each year.[7]) Anger is both a gauge of our progress toward a goal and a force that makes us persist in the face of obstacles.

To me, this all seems quite functional for a sin. And it's this functionality that is leading those of us who study affect to rethink our classification of anger as a negative emotion.

One can get a better understanding of anger's affiliation with the positive emotions by looking at the angry brain. For Charles Carver of the University of Miami and Eddie Harmon-Jones of Texas A&M University, one of the defining features of anger is that it is accompanied by what's called an "approach motivation."[8]

Emotions, as well as other psychological states, such as goals, can be broadly classified as either approach or avoidance. Approach states orient us toward engagement with the environment. They lead us to focus on rewards and incentives and propel us to pursue them. Avoidance states, like fear or disgust, on the other hand, prompt people to distance themselves from aspects of the environment: spiders, for example, or contaminants. The avoidance motivation system is focused on removing threats or punishments.

Each of these motivational orientations has a distinct pattern of brain activation. And it seems that the angry brain looks very much like the approach brain. When you look at the brain under approach motivation, you see a consistent pattern of activation in the left anterior regions of the cortex; when you look at the angry brain, you see much the same thing.[9]

What's even more interesting than the fact that anger motivates approach tendencies is that people recognize that it's a motivator and use it to their advantage.

It is often assumed that emotion regulation is about increasing positive emotions and decreasing negative ones; that people are interested only in feeling good. But this isn't always the case. When you to go to a funeral, for example, it isn't OK to smile inanely or laugh at the eulogy, so you might strategically upregulate sadness and downregulate happiness. You do this because sadness is more appropriate in the funeral context, even though feeling sad is clearly less pleasant than feeling happy.

Something similar applies to anger. Maya Tamir of Boston College and her colleagues, Christopher Mitchell, also at Boston, and James Gross of Stanford, asked participants what kind of music they wanted to listen to before playing a computer game.[10]

The computer game was Soldier of Fortune, a first-person shooter game in which the player walks around a virtual world shooting people. Participants could listen to music that they knew to be neutral in tone, music that was angry, or music that was exciting (but not particularly anger-inducing). These may not be obvious genres, but Tamir tested the tunes beforehand to ensure that they induced the emotions she wanted. Participants got to sample each of the musical pieces before rating how much they would like to listen to it prior to playing the game.

What Tamir and her colleagues found was that people preferred to listen to the angry music before playing Soldier of Fortune. Faced with a task in which anger might serve a useful function, facilitating the shooting of enemies, participants opted for an anger boost. What's more, listening to the angry music actually improved performance, suggesting not only that people strategically regulate anger, but also that such regulation pays off.

Of course, anger is not always a useful emotion. In contexts in which it's not helpful to be competitive (when playing the game Dinner Dash, for example, as other participants in Tamir's study did, in which the goal is quality customer service in a restaurant rather than, well, killing), not only is anger not upregulated, it's actually detrimental to performance. Angry waiters aren't good waiters.

Of course, this is a rather obvious fact. We all know that anger is dysfunctional at times, such as in the service industry or when the vending machine has an unpredictable center of gravity. But the point here is that in the appropriate circumstances, strategically amplifying anger actually makes us perform better.

Angry Minds

The reason anger changes our behaviors is that it changes the way we think. Ironically, it is this very fact that led early anger detractors to demonize the sin. As they saw it, anger's power to distort perception and disturb reason was the heart of the problem. But on closer inspection, it is precisely because anger biases our cognition and perception that it serves us so well.

All emotions are signals of what is important in our immediate surroundings. Fear signals threat, and so encourages people to selectively attend to threatening stimuli, like snakes and spiders, and act in ways to diminish such threats. Anger also selectively biases our attention, but in a different way.

Brett Ford of Boston College brought participants into his lab and gave them an emotion induction much like the one Maya Tamir used in her study on anger and performance.[11] Some participants listened to anger-inducing music and also wrote about a past experience in which they had felt the emotion. Other participants were induced with fear, others with excitement, and yet others, the controls, listened to neutral music and wrote about an emotion-free past event. After emotions were manipulated, participants were hooked up to an eye tracker. By measuring where the eyes are focused during the scanning of an image or text, inferences can be made about what aspects of the environment are capturing people's attention.

While in the eye tracker, Ford's participants were shown pairs of images. Some of these depicted threatening information, like people wielding knives. Others depicted rewarding information, such as people having sex. Others were neutral. There were various combinations of images (threat-reward, threat-neutral, reward-neutral, etc.). After the presentation of each pair of images, a question was asked about a detail of one of the images—for example, "Did you see a key?"

Actually, Ford wasn't interested in the answers to such questions. What he was concerned with was angry people's allocation of attention during image viewing. Given pairs of images, were the angry more likely to focus on threat or reward? On knives or on sex?

There were two possibilities here. Because anger is generally considered a negative emotion and because negative emotions usually direct one's attention to bad stuff in the environment, it was possible that angry participants would selectively attend to the negative, threatening images. But anger, remember, is also an approach emotion, and approach states have been shown to come with a bias toward rewarding information.

So what does anger actually do? When Ford examined where participants spent most of their time looking, he found a clear bias toward rewarding stimuli. It was the erotic couples that seemed most interesting to the angry participants, not the knives. By comparison, and as expected, fearful participants were biased toward threat. Neutral participants showed no bias either way.

The monk John Cassian was afraid that anger would blind us.[12] But it doesn't so much blind us as put a particular brand of functional blinders on our perceptual systems, redirecting them to what is relevant in the environment. When angry, we focus on rewards. And it is this focus that partly explains why we persist in the face of adversity. If we encounter an obstacle while pursuing a goal, anger directs our attention to the rewards of reaching our goal and so breeds perseverance.

Such perceptual shifts are powerful, but they pale against the broader cognitive changes that anger evokes.

Consider the following questions: How likely is it that you will experience the following events during the course of your life?

1. Receiving favorable medical tests at age sixty.
2. Being on an airplane and encountering severe turbulence.
3. Marrying someone wealthy.
4. Developing gum problems.

I don't know what the actual statistics are for these questions, but I do know that how you answer them will depend on how you are currently feeling.

We have known for some time that our current feelings influence how we think and behave. If, for example, you're asked, on a sunny day, how satisfied you are with your life, you'll be more satisfied than if you're asked the same question on a rainy day.[13] The positive mood induced by sunshine makes one more likely to focus on the good things in one's life.

The four questions above, however, are more about risk perception than about general well-being. So what does being angry do to our judgments of risk? To answer this question, psychologists Jennifer Lerner of Harvard and Dacher Keltner of the University of California, Berkeley, recruited some students to do a study, ostensibly on imagination and information processing.[14] When they got to the lab, participants were given one of two sets of instructions. Some were asked to list three to five things that make them very fearful and then to pick the "one situation that makes you, or has made you, most afraid." They had to write about this event with as much vividness and in as much detail as possible, so that someone reading the description might actually become afraid just through reading it. The rest of the participants got the same instructions, except that "angry" replaced "fearful" and "afraid." Although seemingly about imagination, these writing tasks are actually designed to induce the emotions of fear and anger.

After doing this, participants got a list of life events, like the ones in the list, and were asked to rate the likelihood that they would experience each circumstance at some point in their lives. Lerner and Keltner computed an "optimistic risk perception" score from responses to these questions. When they analyzed the results, they found something quite interesting. The emotion that participants happened to be feeling at the time significantly impacted their risk perceptions: Angry people were more optimistic about their futures than were fearful people.

Why does this happen? Lerner and Keltner also measured something else that might give us a clue. Not only did they ask participants how *likely* the events were, but also how *controllable* they were. When they considered the answers to this question, they found that angry people also saw future events as more controllable than did the fearful. The researchers also showed, statistically, that participants were more optimistic because they felt more control.

Such mental shifts are probably what account for the performance benefits attributable to anger. Although our trajectories toward a goal might be momentarily blocked, by focusing on the potential payoff rather than ruminating on our failure, anger prompts us to persist. When we experience this emotion, attention narrows to focus on rewards, and we also have a sense of greater control and optimism, making us think that we can actually attain those rewards.

Open Up and Say Grrrrr

Humans have an amazing capacity for believing weird stuff: that grasping a chicken by the shoulder blades and then shaking your head transfers one's own sins to the chicken; or that about 75 million years ago an intergalactic warlord rounded up a crew of space creatures, flew them to earth, and then dumped them in volcanoes.

Perhaps the only thing that trumps the weirdness of our beliefs is their stubbornness. Once implanted in our brains, beliefs are notoriously hard to change.

Much of our belief resistance is due to what psychologists call the confirmation bias. This is simply what it sounds like, a bias towards confirming what we already believe. And you can see it all around you. It's why Republicans watch Fox News and Democrats watch *The Daily Show*. And it's why first impressions are notoriously hard to shake—we constantly seek information to support them and ignore anything disconfirming.

Now, you might guess that anger, with all its self-righteousness and confidence, would lend itself to stubbornness and increased belief resistance. But there is another possibility. Although anger doesn't routinely lead to violence, it does come with a general behavioral shift toward confrontation. This need not be physical, of course; it may manifest merely as a state of mind. When angry, one might be prone to challenge the views and opinions of others, for example.

This possibility was explored by Maia Young of UCLA in a series of studies.[15] In one of these, participants were asked to indicate their opinion of the effect of hands-free cell phone devices on driving safety. Do hands-free devices reduce the frequency of car accidents? Yes or no? Next, they were given eight statements that were summaries of longer articles on the hands-free debate, ostensibly collected from various media outlets. Participants were asked to read these eight summaries, four of which were clearly pro-hands-free and four of which were anti, and then choose up to five articles that they would like to read in their entirety.

The key manipulation here was what participants were doing before this task. Some were asked to recount as concretely as possible a time in their life when they felt especially angry. Others were asked to write about the events of the previous day; these were the controls.

Control participants showed the typical trend in favor of confirming information: They chose to read articles that confirmed their original position on the issue. But angry participants showed the reverse pattern: They were more likely to select articles containing disconfirming information.

In another of Young's studies, a similar effect was found for political attitudes.[16] When angry participants were asked to select information to read in support of Obama or McCain in the lead-up to the 2008 US presidential election, they showed no confirmation bias: They were just as likely to want to read a piece in support of their preferred candidate as they were to read one favoring the opponent.

The interesting thing about this penchant for disconfirming information is that it may actually open the angry person's mind a little, making her more susceptible to persuasion and attitude change. When Young later asked her participants, after exposure to the five paragraphs, to restate their attitudes to hands-free devices, she found that angry people were indeed more likely than controls to have adjusted their attitudes in the direction of the disconfirming statements.

Part of the reason for such attitude change may be that angry people are processing information more effortfully and analytically. Not only do they *search* for information that might disconfirm their own opinions, they might also *process* this information more carefully. Work by Wesley Moons and Diane Mackie, both from UC Santa Barbara, supports this interpretation, showing that angry people are more sensitive to argument quality, and are persuaded only when disconfirming information is of a high standard.[17]

Note to people on a mission to convert or persuade: annoy your audience first—it opens their minds.

Righteous Anger

One of the best things about being a social psychologist is that, in the name of science, I can get away with exposing unsuspecting participants to things like this:

A man goes to the supermarket once a week and buys a dead chicken. But before cooking the chicken, he has sexual intercourse with it. Then he cooks it and eats it.

Or this:

A brother and sister like to kiss each other on the mouth. When nobody is around, they find a secret hiding place and kiss each other on the mouth, passionately.

These scenarios are used to study moral judgment. They are examples of normative violations, behaviors that transgress certain norms or rules. Some people think these actions, bestial necrophilia and incest, are morally objectionable. I happen not to, and chances are that if you're a liberal from what has recently

been dubbed a WEIRD society (Western, Educated, Industrialized, Rich, and Democratic), then you also don't think these are
morally wrong.[18] You may not be into sex with dead chickens or
making out with your sister and you may even find these things
a little disgusting, but you wouldn't morally condemn someone
for these acts.

Violations like these belong to what Jonathan Haidt, a psychologist at the University of Virginia, calls the "moral domain of
purity."[19] They may violate our sense of the sacred and pure and
produce a feeling of spiritual defilement. Purity, however, is but
one domain among five that comprise the moral universe. According to Haidt, the other four domains are based on harm, fairness,
ingroup loyalty, and social hierarchy.

Different cultures value each of the domains differently. In
WEIRD places like the United States, Australia, and the United
Kingdom, it's really only the harm and fairness domains that are considered in any way morally relevant (unless you're a political conser-
vative, in which case, you tend to moralize all five).[20] In non-WEIRD
cultures, people tend to see all five domains as morally relevant.[21]

So by this account, most of you reading this book would likely
take exception, morally, to the following violations (examples of
harm):

A person puts cyanide in a container of yogurt in a
    supermarket.
Someone steals a purse from a blind woman.

But not only do people deem such behavior morally wrong, they
also feel angry about it. And it's this anger that accounts for their
moral condemnation. According to Haidt, our moral judgments are

driven largely by our emotions and intuitions. And when it comes to violations of rights and fairness, especially those involving harm, it's anger that does the driving.[22]

Anger has evolved as an emotional gauge of injustice. When we see the rights of others trampled or someone get harmed, we get angry. In fact, anger and harm are so closely intertwined that the experience of anger itself may lead us to see harm where none exists. Roberto Gutierrez and Roger Giner-Sorolla of the University of Kent presented participants with the following scenario:[23]

> A man belongs to a necrophilia club that has devised a way to satisfy the desire to have sex with dead people. Each member donates his or her body to the club after death so that the other members of the club can have sex with the corpse. The man has sex with a dead woman who gave her body to the club. She had no surviving family members. The man and all other members of the club use adequate protection so there is no risk of disease being spread. After they are done, they cremate the woman's body, following her final instructions to them.

Those who felt anger about this act were more likely to perceive that someone was harmed. Precisely whom is unclear. Still, the anger-harm link is so ingrained that it biases our perceptions, leading us to impute harm to relatively harmless situations.

So what's the use of all this moral outrage? Sure, we get angry when a person's rights are violated or someone slips a little cyanide into a tub of yogurt, but what is the function of this feeling? As a reaction to goal blockage, anger triggers task persistence.

What does it do in the moral domain? Well, it triggers another kind of approach action.

Imagine the following:

> You come into a lab and you're told you'll be playing a game, a "proposer–responder bargaining" game. In this game, two people, the proposer (your partner) and the responder (you), have to agree on how to split $10. The proposer begins by making you an offer, which you can either accept, in which case you keep the amount offered and the proposer keeps what's left, or reject, in which case you both get nothing.

This is called the "ultimatum game" and it is used to study fairness and self-interest in the laboratory. Now imagine your partner makes you an offer of $4. Would you accept it? What about an offer of $2? If you were being completely rational about the whole thing (and here I mean rational in an economic sense, where all you care about is maximizing your own gain), then you should accept any nonzero offer that the proposer makes. From a purely rational point of view, you should accept an offer of $2 (the proposer keeping the other $8), because $2 is better than nothing. (Indeed, you should accept any offer that is greater than zero; even one cent is technically more than nothing.)

But most people don't behave like this. When Joydeep Srivastava, a professor of marketing at the University of Maryland, and his colleagues asked a group of participants to be responders in the ultimatum game, they found what many other studies have found: that people don't behave like purely rational agents at all.[24] Srivastava split his participants into two groups. Both groups believed they were playing with a real partner, a real proposer, but in fact, the proposals were manipulated by the experimenters. One group was made offers of $2; the other group, $4. Of those offered the reasonable, fair $4, about 80 percent accepted. Of those offered the less-than-fair $2, only about 44 percent took the offer. Over half of these participants refused, in effect punishing the proposer for being unfair.

The interesting thing about Srivastava's study is that researchers considered the role of anger in all this. As you would expect, people in the $2 group considered the offer as significantly less fair than did those in the $4 group. What's more, the $2 participants were much angrier about the offer. And when the researchers did the statistical tests to examine anger's role in people's decisions to accept or reject offers, they found anger indeed led people to reject the unfair offers. Unfairness triggers feelings of indignation and outrage, and as a result, the perpetrator of the unfairness is punished, even though such punishment may come at a cost ($2, in this case).

In the moral domain, as in the performance domain, anger is both a gauge and a trigger. It is an experiential signal that someone's rights are being infringed on or that justice isn't being very well served. It's also a trigger that sets in motion action to redress the perceived wrong. The more anger we feel, the more punishment we seek. The function of moral anger is to uphold certain standards of behavior—those that protect others' rights.

Anger Express

Up to now, we have been considering anger from the inside. We have examined what the *feeling* of anger does for us. But we can also examine anger from the outside. What does *expressing* anger do for us?

In early 1999, just as the US Senate was debating President Bill Clinton's guilt over the Monica Lewinsky scandal, Larissa Tiedens of Stanford University brought two groups of students into her lab to do a study that would have been of use to the Democratic Party's publicity office.[25] One group saw a forty-seven-second clip of Clinton's grand jury testimony, showing an angry Bill Clinton gesticulating with force and staring down the camera barrel as he denounced the behavior of the opposition lawyers. The other group saw a forty-five-second clip of a sadder, more subdued Clinton, with head hung and gaze averted as he discussed the inappropriateness of his relationship with Miss Lewinsky.

After watching these videos, participants reported their agreement with various statements relating to the whole Clinton scandal, such as "Clinton should be removed from office," "The Senate should find Clinton guilty," and "Clinton should be severely punished for his behavior." People who saw the angry Bill were much more in favor of letting the president keep his job and treating him leniently.

Why does this happen? In another of her studies, Tiedens found that anger expressions increased perceptions of competence.[26] We see angry people as dominant, strong, and tough. Presidential qualities, one may argue. Seeing Clinton as angry and thus dominant and presidential led participants to want to keep him in the office his qualities so suitably fit.

This is all fine for Bill Clinton, but what about the rest of us? Those of us who aren't president of the United States, former or otherwise? One possibility is that expressing anger only brings benefits to those already in a position of power. In another study, Tiedens again showed participants one of two video clips, but this time the clips were of a regular person being interviewed for a job.[27] The interviewee in these videos, a male, talked about various things, including a challenging time in his previous job when he and a coworker lost an important client. The two clips were identical, apart from the emotion expressed in response to the lost-client episode: In one video it was anger; in the other, sadness.

After watching the interview, participants answered several questions, including one asking how much the job applicant should be paid. The results show that expressing anger, quite literally, pays: People who saw the angry applicant suggested a salary of $53,700; those who saw the sad applicant; $41,330. This constitutes an anger bonus of just over $12,000.

So what works for Bill Clinton works for the rest of us, right? Well, not quite. Seven years after Bill Clinton's grand jury testimony, Hillary was the Clinton in the news, and social psychologists got another idea for a Clinton family–inspired study. After Mrs. Clinton criticized the Republican Party's behavior in Congress, Ken Mehlman, chairman of the Republican National Committee, criticized her right back about being angry.[28] In a commentary on the episode, *New York Times* columnist Maureen Dowd wrote the following:

> They are casting Hillary Clinton as an Angry Woman, a she-monster melding images of Medea, the Furies, harpies. . . . This gambit handcuffs Hillary: If she doesn't speak out strongly against President Bush, she's timid and girlie. If she does, she's a witch and a·shrew.[29]

So when Bill is angry, he's presidential and unimpeachable, but when Hillary gets riled up, she's a witch?

To test the idea that anger expressions may backfire for

women, Victoria Brescoll of Yale and Eric Uhlmann of North-western University replicated Tiedens's job interviewee study, but used female in addition to male interviewees.[30] Again, angry men got a salary bump: $37,807 for the angry versus $30,033 for the sad. But women paid an anger penalty of about $5,500: Suggested salaries were $23,464 for the angry, $28,970 for the sad.

Why do women pay an anger penalty? It's because of how the emotion is explained. For men, anger is expected, it's normal, and when it's expressed, it is seen to be triggered by external cues: The printer broke or my wife cheated on me, so I'm pissed. Anger is seen as an appropriate response to environmental triggers.

But for women, stereotyped as the caring, softer, and kinder sex, anger seems unusual, and as a result, it tends to be attributed to internal, dispositional causes. Angry women are seen as just that: inherently angry women. There is good news for the angry woman, however: If your anger is attributed not to who you are but to environmental triggers, then the anger penalty disappears.

Negotiating Anger

I hate dealing with phone companies. I don't do it very often, but when I do, it's invariably a frustrating experience. It all begins when you dial the number and are connected to Lara or Sarah or some other automated and always female voice recording who regales you with a range of possible reasons for your call. "Bill inquiry?" "Change of address?" You respond with a yes or a no and the voice recognition software that's meant to decode these elaborate responses doesn't work. "No." "Was that yes? Press 1 to confirm." Your frustration rises but you try to remain civil. You keep your composure for a few rounds of this farcical back and forth until you either give up and hang up, or Lara decides to connect you to a real person.

I've always wondered why phone companies insist on infuriating their customers in this way. But from the customers' point of view, this naturalistic anger induction might actually pay off, especially if they're trying to negotiate something.

In a study by Gerben van Kleef, Carsten De Dreu, and Antony Manstead at the University of Amsterdam, participants took the role of a mobile phone salesperson and were asked to negotiate with a buyer over the price, warranty period, and service contract duration of a consignment of phones.[31] The negotiation would be computer mediated, so they would type their offers into dialogue boxes and be able to view the offers and comments of their negotiation partner, the buyer, in similar boxes on the screen. Their goal was to get the best deal possible. In fact, participants were negotiating not with a real buyer, but with a computer, programmed to make a preset series of offers over the course of six bargaining rounds. The details of this negotiation paradigm are a little complicated and they don't really matter for our purposes; the important point is that the participants (i.e., the sellers) were led to believe that the "buyer" (i.e., the computer) was feeling happy or angry or emotionally neutral about the progress of the negotiation.

As the negotiation rolled on, offers and counteroffers appearing in dialogue boxes, there appeared the occasional comment from the buyer. In one condition, the buyer seemed rather calm, offering bland and emotionally neutral comments like, "I think I'll offer $115 for the phones, with a six-month warranty and a seven-month contract." In another condition, the buyer gave the impression of being happy about the whole thing: "This is going pretty well so far; I think I'll offer . . ." In the third condition, however, the buyer didn't seem happy at all: "I am going to offer $115 for the phones, with a six-month warranty and a seven-month contract, because this negotiation pisses me off."

The researchers were interested in how the buyers' emotional reactions would influence the demands made by the seller. Would anger simply fuel the fire, ramping up seller anger and increasing the competitiveness of the negotiation? Or would angry buyers scare sellers into backing off? It was the second of these possibilities that occurred: Sellers who faced an angry buyer made lower demands and were happier to make concessions than those with happy or neutral opponents.

This happens because anger expressions signal competence, ambition, and toughness, all factors that suggest that a negotiator knows what he's doing and might be a fierce competitor.[32]

But there are a couple of important caveats to using anger in negotiation:

1. Don't try it on the powerful. If you express anger to a negotiating partner who is of higher status than you, it won't work as well.[33]
2. Don't try it in Asia. Different cultures have different rules—called emotional display rules—for when and how it is appropriate to express emotions. And although it's fine to express anger in the United States and other Western cultures, it's not done in many Eastern cultures. In countries like Japan, which place a significant premium on social harmony and interdependence, it's not appropriate

to display anger. So if Asian negotiators find themselves facing an angry buyer or seller, they may not only not concede, but actually retaliate.[34]

Angry Couples

Anger may work for us in a negotiation context in which we're trying to maximize our own gains at the expense of others, but what does it do in that very different kind of negotiating context, the romantic relationship? This is an important question, as the majority of our anger experiences occur with people we like or love.[35] In fact, about half of our anger episodes occur in the home.[36]

Conventional wisdom has it that anger is destructive to relationships. But the empirical evidence tells a different story. In a study by Howard Kassinove of Hofstra University and his colleagues, when about 750 people were asked to think about recent anger episodes in close relationships, over half (55 percent) reported positive outcomes.[37]

What seems to matter most for anger's success in the relationship arena is how it's experienced and expressed. In another study by Kassinove and his colleagues Raymond Tafrate and Louis Dundin of Central Connecticut State University, people who experienced dysfunctional thinking patterns during their anger episode (including things like being excessively demanding and blaming) reported worse outcomes.[38] These thought patterns are associated with a set of even more dysfunctional behaviors, such as yelling and screaming, which do nothing to help the situation. But those who experienced anger in the absence of these dysfunctional thoughts and behaviors were twice as likely to report long-term positive outcomes.

It really comes down to how anger is expressed. If the focus

is on calmly discussing the reasons for one's rage, then the outcome is often good. Part of this constructive response involves
recognizing one's own faults. Although angry people are often
deemed irrational and self-righteous, recall that the research suggests that they may in fact be open-minded, and more likely than
the nonangry to search for evidence disconfirming their current
beliefs. This is a likely contributor to successful outcomes in close
relationships.

In her 1993 essay on the sin, novelist Mary Gordon describes her-
self in the grip of anger:

> I lost it. I lost myself. I jumped on the hood of the car.
> I pounded on the windshield. I told my mother and my
> children that I was never, ever going to take any of them
> anywhere and none of them were ever going to have one
> friend in any house of mine until the hour of their death,
> which, I said, I hoped was soon.[39]

What we've seen in this chapter is that none of this windshield
pounding is actually inherent in anger. Far from it. Rather, the
mind-set that comes with the emotion is a functional response to
challenges in the environment. Whether a response to goal blockage or injustice, anger promotes adaptive behavioral strategies:
persistence, optimism, control, punishment. Of course, if anger
grips us too tightly, it may morph these adaptive responses into
the maladaptive—persistence into stubbornness, optimism into
unwarranted riskiness, control into obsession, and punishment
into vengeance. As with the other sins, anger must be exercised
with caution and a little restraint.

Envy: How Wanting What Others Have Makes You Happier, Smarter, and More Creative

In Ovid's *Metamorphoses* the goddess Envy lives in a shack, eats snakes, has black teeth, and oozes bile out of parts of her body it's probably best not to mention. It's no wonder envy has a bad name. But when people refer to the sin in everyday conversation, they often don't have in mind anything like the corrupt, bile-dripping brand of envy portrayed by Ovid.

One of the most influential psychological definitions of this sin comes from the work of W. Gerrod Parrott of Georgetown University and Richard Smith of the University of Kentucky: "Envy occurs when a person lacks another's superior quality, achievement, or possession, and either desires it or wishes that the other lacks it."[1] And while other psychologists have been a little more creative with their definitions, grounding envy in childhood longings for penises and breasts, it's the more mundane, body-part-neutral description of Parrott and Smith's that holds sway in modern, mainstream psychology.

In this definition we can clearly see that envy has two

meanings. In the first, the envier lacks what another has and simply wants it. A guy in a Ferrari 599 GTB pulls up next to you at the traffic lights and you think, "Ah, nice car. I want one." Nothing too insidious here. In the second sense of the sin, the envier lacks what another has, but this time wants the other not to have it: "Ah, nice car. Wouldn't it be great if a semitrailer plowed into the back of it." The first kind is the good kind, what we psychologists call benign envy; the second, not-so-pleasant brand, which is a close relative of resentment, we call malicious envy. And it probably won't surprise you that I'll be focusing on the benign variety in this chapter.

(Another definitional point to clear up: "Envy" and "jealousy" are often used interchangeably; they are not the same thing to psychologists. Envy involves wanting something that another person possesses—some quality or object. This is a two-person affair: the envier and the envied person, as well as the envied object or attribute. In other words: you, the guy in the Ferrari, and the Ferrari itself. Jealousy, however, is a three-way affair. I'm jealous of someone if they pose a threat of stealing another person away from me. I'm jealous of Ferrari guy if he makes a move on my girlfriend. Three people are involved here: me, Ferrari guy, and girlfriend. Jealousy is not the topic of this chapter.)

For social psychologists, envy is all about what we call "social comparison." In 1954, social psychologist Leon Festinger put forward a rather elaborate, yet elegantly simple theory of this ubiquitous psychological process.[2] The elaborate part is the nine hypotheses, eight corollaries, and eight derivations that make up his classic paper. The elegantly simple part is this: When people are uncertain about their own abilities or attitudes, they compare themselves to others. We all engage in such comparison, all the time. Is she more attractive than I am? Taller? Shorter? Fatter? Smarter? Richer? Wiser? Much of what we know, think, believe, and value is known, thought, believed, and valued in comparison to other people.

Now, logically, social comparison can go in three directions: up, down, or sideways. Envy, of course, is all about the upward variety; it's about comparing ourselves to those better off. In his famous essay on the sin, philosopher Francis Bacon noted that "deformed persons and eunuchs and old men and bastards are envious."[3] This may be true, but they're not the only ones. It turns out that the upward comparison so central to envy is quite common indeed. In fact, social comparison is so central a part of our lives that we often do it spontaneously, without intending to.[4] Common it may be, but what precisely is all this envious upward comparison good for?

Feels Good

We've all heard that piece of folk wisdom: There's always someone worse off than you. And although this is technically true for all but one of us, the intuition that we must compare downward in order to feel better about ourselves doesn't always prove true. In fact, in many cases, it is upward comparison that does a better job of improving our moods.

Starting college is a rather stressful experience. You have all the pressures of the first semester of class, of working out the complexities of your schedule, of settling in to dorm life, and so on. Imagine that you're about halfway through your freshman year and you learn that you'll be getting a new roommate. And imagine, unlikely as it may sound, that you get a choice: Rebecca or Stacey. Rebecca, you learn, is coping quite well with college life:

She has easily adjusted to being away from home, has made plenty of friends, and is doing very well in class. Stacey, on the other hand, isn't coping so well. She is homesick, has had a hard time making friends, and is not faring too well in her courses. Which roommate would be a more sensible choice? The enviable Rebecca, or poor old Stacey?

Lisa Aspinwall and Shelley Taylor, then both at UCLA, ran a study getting at a similar question.[5] They brought college undergraduates into their lab and exposed them to a Rebecca or to a Stacey, to a successful or unsuccessful comparison target. When these researchers later measured participants' mood, they found that those exposed to a successful Rebecca type felt better than those who compared downward, to a less successful target. When Aspinwall and Taylor probed the results a little further, they found that such mood boosts coincided with feelings of hope. The enviable, successful student shows the rest of us that, yes, it can be done. That we too can do well in class and have friends. And this sense of hope makes us feel better.

There's an even simpler means by which envious upward comparison makes us feel better about ourselves: when we size ourselves up against someone better off, we actually come to view ourselves as more similar to them and thus in a more positive light.

The classic demonstration of this comes from a study by Ladd Wheeler of Macquarie University in Sydney.[6] In what has come to be known as the rank-order paradigm, Wheeler first gave participants a basic task. Then, being a true social psychologist, he provided false feedback. He gave subjects a score on the task, told them their ranking, and made it clear that they'd performed at an average level, falling somewhere in the middle of the distribution. Next he gave participants a rank-ordered list of other people who had done the same task. He told participants that they could look at the score of any person on the list.

The question Wheeler was interested in was, To whom would participants compare themselves? They could choose someone worse off, or someone ranked higher. What he found was that 87 percent of people chose to compare themselves to someone who performed better. Upward comparison was the norm.

But the really interesting part of this study is what came next. When Wheeler asked participants to indicate how similar they were to the person they had chosen to compare themselves to, he discovered that those who compared up tended to see themselves as similar to their comparison targets. According to Wheeler, these envious participants were trying to confirm that they were "almost as good as the very good ones." The participants who didn't compare up had accepted their inferiority, judging themselves as similar to those below them.

Another study by Penelope Lockwood and Ziva Kunda, then both at the University of Waterloo, Canada, makes this point even more clearly.[7] Female undergraduate students at Waterloo with career aspirations of being teachers were recruited for a study on "the effects of journalistic styles on social perception." Some students read a fake newspaper article describing a female teacher who had recently won an award for outstanding career achievement. This teacher worked in an inner city high school, had met difficult challenges with enthusiasm, and was adept at motivating her students. She was described as being "one of the most talented, creative, and innovative teachers" that her school principal had ever worked with. A target of envy, without doubt.

After reading this article, the would-be teachers next answered some questions about themselves, allegedly to ensure that their personality characteristics wouldn't bias their perceptions of the article. They rated themselves on intelligence, skill, and competence, among other traits. The researchers were interested not in how these ratings would influence perceptions of the article, but in how reading the article would influence these very ratings. So did comparing oneself to a successful other somehow boost one's self-image, making these would-be teachers view themselves as more talented and creative, just like the teacher in the article? It sure did. Students who compared themselves to this inspirational teacher rated themselves as more bright and skillful and less incompetent than did students who made no such comparison. Making this upward comparison quite literally changed these students' evaluations of their own personality characteristics.

There is a final way, in addition to promoting hope and creating a positive self-image, that envy can make us feel better.

Consider this choice. You can either: (1) have dinner at a fancy restaurant this coming weekend and then eat at home for the following two weekends or (2) eat at home this weekend, go to the fancy restaurant next weekend, and then eat at home the weekend after that.

Which option would you choose? If you're like 84 percent of respondents, you'd choose option 2, the *home-fancy-home* option. Why?[8]

When economists talk about the value of things—of goods or of experiences—they talk about "utility." This is just a technical way of describing the amount of satisfaction or happiness one derives from something. Now if you think about options 1 and 2 above, at first glance they seem to have the same utility; both options involve one fancy dinner out and two dinners at home.

So why do so many people choose option 2? It's because option 2 has a kind of utility that option 1 lacks. Both have the same *consumption* utility—they involve the same experiences, which when consumed should bring the same amount of satisfaction. But by delaying the expensive dinner for a week (as in option 2), one can derive pleasure from the very act of *anticipating* this special experience. Option 2 has *anticipation utility*; option 1 does not. And so overall, option 2 brings more satisfaction.

You find a similar preference for the delay of valued experiences in a study by the behavioral economist George Loewenstein of Carnegie Mellon University.[9] When Loewenstein asked college students how much they would pay for a kiss from their favorite movie star, he found that students were willing to pay more to be kissed in three days' time than they were to be kissed immediately. Even though the consumption utility would be the same for an immediate and a delayed kiss, the anticipation utility of the delayed kiss brings pleasure in itself and so ups the amount one is willing to pay.

Now envy, by its very nature, is steeped in anticipation utility. One of the central characteristics of the emotion is a sense of longing, that feeling of "if only I had what she has."[10] The envier simulates what life would be like with the envied object or attribute, and this simulation itself brings pleasure.

Blessed Are the Envious, for They Shall Be Smarter and More Creative

I want you to take a minute and think about as many possible uses for a brick as you can. Not the run-of-the-mill, boring uses (building houses, throwing through windows), but weird, unusual, creative uses.

Psychologists ask people questions like this, about bricks and other things, to assess creativity. This is an example of what is

called an "alternative uses task." The more original and elaborate
one's listed uses, the more creative one is deemed to be. (The best
weird brick use I've ever come across: "mock coffin at a Barbie funeral," although "hitting my sister in the head" is a close second.)

What does any of this have to do with envy? Well, envy can
actually make you more creative. In a study by Camille Johnson of
Stanford and Diederik Stapel of Tilburg University, students came
into the lab to do a test of "integrative orientation intelligence."[11]
At least that's what these unwitting subjects were told. In fact, the
researchers were actually interested in the impact of social comparison processes on creativity. When participants first arrived at
the lab, some read a description of a successful peer who routinely
scored in the top 5 percent of his classes, was popular, and had
lots of friends. This person served as a comparison target—an
obviously enviable, upward comparison target for most. Participants in another condition, the control condition, read an unin-
spiring article about the university campus. Next, participants did
the brick uses task. And, once again proving that envy is not all
bile and black teeth, the envious, upwardly comparing participants
were more creative, thinking of more things to do with a brick
than the controls.

So, just as one *evaluates* oneself as more talented when comparing to an envied other, one also *becomes* more talented. But such
behavioral effects aren't restricted to creativity.

Hart Blanton of the University at Albany and some of his colleagues examined the effects of social comparison in that cauldron
of envy: the classroom.[12] These researchers kept tabs on about
nine hundred Dutch schoolkids for a year. What Blanton and his
colleagues were interested in was the kids' grades: How well did
they perform in biology, French, math? But they were also inter-

ested in the ways in which students compared themselves to others. One might imagine that kids would take every opportunity to
compare downward in an attempt to feel better about their own
academic abilities. But this is not what Blanton found. The typical
student actually compared up. Just as with adults, for schoolkids,
envious comparison is the norm.

But the even more interesting outcome is what such upward
comparisons did to students' grades. Over the course of the year,
comparing upward to their better-performing classmates improved students' grades. And such results are not limited to the
classroom. We see similar performance benefits in the lab, when
people perform tedious reaction time tasks with superior partners,
or when women are given a math test by a competent rather than
incompetent female experimenter.[13]

How does social comparison work here? There are a few reasons why envy might make us smarter and more creative.

First, comparison can provide information on how a task is
done. If you have the good fortune to observe a skilled performer,
you watch, you learn, and so you perform better.

Second, envy can change your expectations about what it is
possible to achieve. In other words, it can change your perceived
likelihood of success. For example, business students who read
about a successful business major forecast higher salaries for
themselves than those who read about an unsuccessful student.[14]
Exposure to the successful role model gave these students hope
that they too could achieve similar financial success.

And third, envying a role model might simply increase your
general motivation to do well.

Hopefully you are starting to see that envy isn't as bad as Ovid
makes out. But neither is it a foolproof means of self-enhancement

and self-improvement. In some circumstances, envy can go horribly wrong. To avoid the pitfalls of envying badly, one needs to be cautious both of whom and of what one is envious.

Who Would Envy an Accountant?

To whom we compare ourselves matters a lot. Typically, people are in the habit of envying those *slightly* better than themselves, but you can't take just any old better-than-you target and hope that envying him will pay off. Your idol needs to be someone *similar* to you. And one thing that determines similarity is the social category to which a comparison target belongs.

Remember the study by Penelope Lockwood and Ziva Kunda in which aspiring teachers judged themselves as smarter and more skilled after comparing themselves to an inspirational role model? Well, these researchers got another group of teaching students to compare themselves not to a successful teacher, but to a successful accountant.[15] These subjects read an article describing the achievements of a high-flying accountant who had become one of the youngest partners ever in her firm and who was described by her boss as an extraordinary and innovative individual. When participants were then asked to rate their own competence and intelligence, upward comparison made no difference. For upward comparison to work, you have to get the category right.

But simply getting the category right isn't always enough. Yes, teachers should envy teachers, and accountants should envy accountants, but not any old teacher or accountant will do. Once you've hit on the right social category (teacher or accountant), you have to pick the right exemplar. Teachers need to choose the right teacher to envy.

What determines the right exemplar? One key factor is that

the person you envy has to have qualities, achievements, or goods that are *attainable*.

In another study by Lockwood and Kunda, budding accountants this time were exposed to a fake newspaper article about an outstanding fourth-year accountancy student, Jennifer Walker.[16] Ms. Walker had a superb academic record and also excelled in extracurricular activities, sports, community service, and so on. And just as in Lockwood and Kunda's teacher/accountant study, after reading this article, participants rated themselves on a set of attributes relating to career success. The catch here, however, was that some of the budding accountants exposed to this actuarial superstar were *first-year* accountancy students, whereas others were *fourth-year* students. For the first years, accountancy superstardom was, at least in principle, still attainable. If they remained focused on their studies and worked hard enough, then they could be the next Jennifer Walker. But for the fourth-year students, already at Jennifer's career stage, such achievements were out of reach. These students had no time to become the next Ms. Walker. When Lockwood and Kunda analyzed the results, they found that this difference in attainability had a big impact on self-evaluations: First-year students, for whom success was still achievable, were buoyed by reading about Jennifer's achievements; fourth-year students were not.

The moral of the story here is straightforward: If you're in the mood for feeling better about yourself, envy someone whose qualities you can achieve.

The Right Stuff

Envying the wrong kind of person is one pitfall; another is envying the wrong kind of stuff. You may covet your neighbor's wife or his recent lottery win, and you may, as a result, try to get your hands on a wife or some lottery tickets of your own. But chances are that, even if you do go out and get what you want, you won't be all that satisfied once you have it. Don't worry, you're not alone. It turns out that most of us are notoriously bad at predicting what will make us happy.

There are a number of reasons why people don't get their happiness predictions right. A central problem is that we tend to overestimate the longevity of our positive emotions. This is partly because when predicting the emotional future, we concentrate on certain key events or objects and fail to take into account everything else that could potentially influence happiness.

Think about your favorite sports team winning an important match. How happy would you be in the days following the victory? When Timothy Wilson of the University of Virginia asked college students just this question, he discovered a clear tendency to mispredict: People thought that a win would produce longer-lasting happiness than it in fact did.[17] The reason for this is that people tended to concentrate on the event itself (the sporting win) and failed to appreciate that in the days following the win they'd be engaged in the banalities of going to class, doing the dishes, and a host of other mundane activities that would distract them from the victory and so dilute their happiness.

The simple fact is that people fail to realize that they will adapt to whatever happens to them. Your football team wins and you are happy for a while, but you adapt. You win the lottery, but then you focus on other things.[18] You get married, and, yes, you adapt.[19]

The point here is that you should be careful in envying your neighbors their married lives and lottery wins, because these things probably won't bring as much happiness as you expect. I'm not saying that lotteries and marriage won't bring a rush of emotion when they first happen. Of course they do. The point to remember is that this happiness often fades with time.

But the good news is that some factors slow the process of adaptation. It turns out that we tend to adapt to things more quickly if they are stable, predictable, and certain. However, if events are unstable, variable, and uncertain, adaptation slows, and we get more happiness for longer.

In one clever study, Jaime Kurtz of the University of Virginia, along with Timothy Wilson and Harvard social psychologist Daniel Gilbert, brought participants into the lab to do an experiment about the effectiveness of website designs.[20] At the beginning of the session participants learned that one in five of them would win a prize. They were given a list of the prizes offered: a camera, a box of chocolates, a mug, and so on. They were then asked to pick their two favorite prizes. Next, participants played a virtual roulette-style game that would determine whether they were one of the lucky winners. (Although participants believed they had only a one-in-five chance of winning, the game was, in fact, rigged such that everyone won.)

The key manipulation came next. Some subjects immediately played another game to determine which of their two favored prizes they would actually win. They spun another virtual roulette wheel, which randomly landed on one of their two preferred prizes. Other participants, however, were told that they wouldn't find out which prize they had won until the end of the experiment.

The researchers were interested in how participants' happiness levels would change over time depending on this manipulation. What we have here is a manipulation of certainty. Those who immediately discovered the identity of their prize were certain of what they had won. Those who had to wait until the experiment's end were uncertain. As expected, all participants were fairly happy when they initially discovered that they would win something. However, the interesting finding was that those participants who had to wait until the end of the study to find out which prize they had won, and were thus in a state of uncertainty, had longer-lasting happiness (as measured by self-reported mood questionnaires) than those who immediately became aware of which prize they would get.

Uncertain events produce lasting happiness because they are harder to "ordinize."[21] When people have an emotional experience, positive or negative, they try to make sense of it, they try to make it "ordinary," and as a result its emotional impact is dampened. Wilson calls this the "pleasure paradox": People try to rationalize and understand positive events so that they can control them and increase their predictability, but in doing so they attenuate the very pleasure they're trying to maximize.[22] Thus, the paradox.

So, yes, uncertainty matters for adaptation. But so does variability.

I like wine. I have a friend who has a very impressive cellar, and I am quite envious of him. Let's say this envy motivates me to go out and stock my own cellar with something better than the ten-dollar stuff I usually buy. What strategy should I use here? Let's say I have $500 to spend. I can go out and buy seven bottles of $44 wine and three bottles of better quality $64 wine, or I can buy three bottles of $36 wine and seven bottles of $56 wine. (I could of course do other things, but I'm trying to make a point here.) Which is a better investment? Which set of ten wines am I more likely to enjoy?

At first glance it might seem that the second option is the

better one. Here I'm more frequently consuming a higher quality wine and only occasionally resorting to the cheaper $36 variety. The occasional cheaper wine reminds me of just how good the more expensive wine is, which makes me appreciate the $56 wine all the more. And this is what a lot of psychology research shows us: People are happier in situations in which there are frequent high-value options and fewer low-value options.[23]

However, there's an important caveat here. If I come to *expect* to drink expensive wine, then the second option might actually turn out to be worse. If I view the expensive, $56 wine as the *norm*, and the cheaper $36 wine as an exception, then when I drink the more expensive wine, my expectations are met and it doesn't really bring all that much pleasure. But when I drink the cheaper wine, my expectations aren't met, and so I experience displeasure. If I do indeed come to view the more frequent experience as the norm, then the first option is actually better. Here, the norm is the cheaper $44 bottle, and when I drink it, my expectations are met. The exception is the more expensive $64 bottle, which exceeds my expectations and brings me more satisfaction.[24]

The point in all this is that you should be careful what you wish for. We aren't very good at predicting what makes us happy and so the objects of envy might not change our lives in the ways we expect. But there are ways around this. Inject a little uncertainty and appropriate variability into your envied experiences once acquired, and you'll be well on the way to getting the most out of them.

Ambient Temperature Is a Girl's Best Friend

What's the difference between bathwater and a diamond? This is not a trick question. There are some obvious differences, of course:

Bathwater is, well, water, and a diamond isn't. But there is one very important distinction that needs to be appreciated if we are to envy well. And it's a distinction that Christopher Hsee (pronounced "shee"), a behavioral economist at the University of Chicago, is very familiar with.

In a study conducted with numerous colleagues in psychology and marketing, Hsee recruited 136 female students from a university in China.[25] When these students arrived at the lab, they were, unbeknownst to themselves, assigned to one of two groups: a "poor" group and a "rich" group. Depending on the group they were in, participants were given goods of different value to compare. In the poor group, each person was paired with another poor group member and each pair was given two diamonds: One person in the pair got a 3-millimeter diamond; the other, a 4.4-millimeter diamond. They were asked to compare their diamonds and then, while holding their diamond in their hand, to indicate how happy they would feel wearing a ring with a setting of that size. People in the rich group did exactly the same thing, but their two diamonds were bigger: One was 5.8 millimeters in diameter, the other 7.2.

When Hsee and his colleagues examined predicted happiness ratings, they found that only *relative* diamond size mattered. Within each group, the person with the larger diamond was happier. Participants *within* groups could compare their diamonds with each other and as a result based their happiness on their relative standing within groups. However, there was no average difference in happiness *between* the poor and rich groups. Even though those in the rich group had larger diamonds, they were no happier than those in the poor group. So for diamonds, it appears happiness depends on comparison, not on absolute size.

These "poor" and "rich" participants were also asked to make another comparison: this time not between diamonds, but between bottles of water. Much like the diamond situation, pairs of participants in the poor and rich groups were given two bottles of water. In the poor group, one member got a bottle of 54°F water and the other, a 72°F bottle. Pairs in the rich group got 90°F and 108°F bottles. Partners were then encouraged to compare their bottles and rate how happy they would feel taking a bath in water of the same temperature as that in their bottle.

A very different happiness pattern emerged here. Unlike in the diamond case, for water temperature, people in the rich group (those with 90°F and 108°F bottles) predicted greater happiness than those in the poor group. In fact, when Hsee looked at happiness ratings across groups, he found a linear increase as a function of temperature: 108°F produced greater happiness than 90°F, which in turn produced greater happiness that 72°F, which in turn produced greater happiness than 54°F. What this suggests is that the pleasure that temperature brings is not relative, but absolute. Because participants did not have the opportunity to compare between groups, the resulting happiness differences can't be based on comparison.

This study examined predicted rather than actual happiness. To address this shortcoming, Hsee did a follow-up field study in which 6,951 people in thirty-one of mainland China's major cities were contacted for a phone survey.[26] The researchers asked each person a number of questions, four of which are pertinent here:

1. How happy do you feel when you think about the present temperature of your room?
2. How happy do you feel when you think about your jewelry (watches included)?

3. What is the present temperature of your room?
4. How much is your jewelry worth?

You can think about this study as a larger version of the diamonds and bathwater experiment. Here diamonds are replaced
with jewelry, and water temperature with ambient room temperature. When Hsee analyzed the results, he found a consistent pattern. Just as diamond-based happiness depended on comparison,
so too did jewelry-based happiness. *Within* cities, those with more
valuable jewelry felt happier. People are likely to compare their
own jewelry with that of other people living in the same city and
thus derive comparison-based happiness. But between cities, jewelry value made no difference: Those cities with higher average
jewelry values were not happier cities.

The pattern of results for room temperature was again strik-
ingly different. Yes, within cities, those in warmer rooms were happier, but this difference emerged at the city level, too: Cities with
higher average room temperatures had happier citizens.

The key difference then, between bathwater and diamonds (and
between room temperature and jewelry) is the difference between
absolute and relative happiness. Ambient temperature increases absolute happiness, not relative happiness. This is because the pleasure
of a warm bath is independent of what anyone else is doing or experiencing. If we're warm, we're happy, and we're not any less happy
if the guy down the street is also warm. Comparison doesn't matter
for temperature. And it shouldn't matter for other things, like sleep,
for which we have innate, physiological scales for assessing where
we stand. If I'm tired, I know it; I don't need to compare myself to
anyone else to get this information. And if I get enough sleep, I'm
happy. I'm no happier if my neighbor is sleeping longer than I am.

But we don't have internal scales for measuring diamond size or jewelry value. The joy we derive from a 3-millimeter diamond depends on the size of the diamonds that those around us have. If someone has a bigger diamond, we're not as happy.

There are two basic lessons to take from this when it comes to envy. First, it's generally a good bet to envy others their ambient temperatures and similar goods. If your envy drives you to acquire such things, you can ensure happiness regardless of what those around you have.

There is of course more to life than just sleep and temperature. We will inevitably envy others their cars, houses, and all manner of other things whose value we can only gauge through comparison to others. These aren't the best things to envy because we'll only be happy with them if our cars and houses are bigger than our neighbors.' So the second point to note: if you must envy others goods that influence *relative* happiness, then once you get your hands on such goods, be sure to compare downward. Our shiny new Ford will make us happy when we compare it to the less shiny, older Buick that our neighbor drives. If we compare it to the Ferrari across the street, we won't feel so good about our new purchase.

There are quite a few tricks to envying well, not least of which are choosing the right people and the right stuff to envy. Add a little variability and a little uncertainty in the right places and you're well on the way to not only feeling better but perhaps actually becoming a little smarter or more creative. Choose poorly, however—wrong people, wrong stuff, wrong kinds of variability, and overly certain outcomes—and you may end up bearing more of a resemblance to Ovid's bile-oozing Envy than you might like.

CHAPTER 7

Pride: That Which Cometh Before
Quite a Lot of Good Stuff

Pride sits atop the list of seven deadly sins; it is an honor that is thoroughly undeserved. Pride is the dullest of the seven. It doesn't have the sexiness of lust, the riskiness of anger, or the blatant excesses of greed and gluttony. The proud aren't dangerous or even very interesting. They are, if anything, simply annoying. So why number one?

Sensibly, it wasn't always so. Pride has a rather strange history as a deadly sin. First of all, pride used to be two sins (pride and vainglory), not one, and although both were featured on early writers' lists of nasty vices, they never fared very well in the rankings. The prides ranked sixth and seventh on the fourth-century list of the monk Evagrius Ponticus, barely scraping in at all. But in A.D. 590, Pope Gregory upped pride's sinfulness by dubbing it the source from which all the other vices derived their wickedness. In fact, Gregory thought pride too insidious to rank with other deadlies, so he actually took it off the list, christening it both the root of all evil and the queen of sin. Vainglory, pride's sibling, jumped to the number one spot. After a while someone got tired of the confusion (the difference between pride and vainglory was never clearly understood) and simply collapsed the two into plain old pride and sat it at the top of the list.[1]

At the heart of all this *general* confusion—worst sin of all or just deadly? one sin or two?—is a more *specific* confusion about definitions. When people think about pride they usually have one of two meanings in mind. And it's the difference between pride's two senses that makes all the difference in pride's status as a sin.

How similar in meaning are these words?

  Cocky and arrogant
  Confident and victorious
  Pretentious and achieving

Jessica Tracy, a psychologist at the University of British Columbia, and Richard Robins of the University of California at Davis asked a group of students precisely this question about these word pairs and many others.[2] The pairs—which also included words like "self-confident," "egotistic," "conceited," and "haughty"—were sampled from some of Tracy and Robins's previous work and were chosen because they bear some resemblance to pride. When the similarity ratings were in, the researchers did some statistical analyses to try to uncover the hidden structure in the way people think about pride. Two clusters emerged.

In one we find:

  triumphant
  victorious
  accomplish
  confident
  winner

And in the other:

arrogant
stuck-up
egotistic
boastful

The first kind of pride, marked by worthy achievement and success, Tracy and Robins called *authentic pride*. The second, with all its conceitedness and arrogance, they called *hubristic pride*.

This distinction is not particularly new—Aristotle hit on something quite similar in his *Nicomachean Ethics*—but Tracy and Robins's demonstration was the first systematic, scientific exploration of the distinction.[3] And this matters. The definitions that philosophers and psychologists use often don't match up with the definitions that everyone else uses. (Think of guilt and shame, for example, or envy and jealousy—concepts often used synonymously by laypeople but considered quite distinct by psychologists.) For pride, however, there was a match.

What is even more interesting is that these two kinds of pride spring from predictable and different causes. Consider the following. How would you feel if:

You recently had an important exam and you studied hard for it. You just found out that you did very well on the exam.

And how would you feel in this scenario:

You've always been naturally talented. You recently
had an important exam and you didn't bother studying
much for it, but it still seemed very easy to you. You just
found out that you did very well on the exam.

If you're anything like participants in another of Tracy and
Robins's studies, you'd feel authentic pride in the first case and
hubristic pride in the second.[*] Why? It turns out that the different prides come from different ways of appraising or explain-
ing events. Interestingly, it's not the *kind* of event that matters;
whether it's grades, athletic performance, personal achievements, or relationship success makes no difference. What does
matter is how you explain such successes. Both kinds of pride
come from seeing a positive event as central to one's goals and
identity and, importantly, as being caused by the self. But when
an important success is attributed to effort and hard work, authentic pride is the result; your pride here is proportional and
well earned. When success is attributed to more stable and
global causes, like ability or talent, however, it's cocky hubris
that tends to follow.

So much for where the two prides come from. But we're more
interested in the consequences of the seven deadly sins and how
we can use them to our advantage. So what does authentic pride
do for us? What does hubris do? And are these incarnations of this
queen of all sins good or bad?

To Pride Oneself on Hard Work

In 1993, Gore Vidal was asked to write an essay on pride for a
collection of short literary pieces on the deadly sins. Vidal was a
sensible choice. Writer Martin Amis once noted that "if there is a

key to Gore Vidal's public character, it has something to do with his towering immodesty, the enjoyable superbity of his self-love."[5] But on sitting down to write the essay, Vidal was a bit puzzled by the concept of pride as a sin. So obvious were pride's virtues to Vidal that he began the essay: "Is pride a sin at all?"[6]

With Vidal we might concede some of the obvious merits of pride (this is authentic pride, now, the good kind). It's associated with the better bits of personality: The authentically proud are more extroverted, more agreeable, more emotionally stable, conscientious, and open to new experiences. The list goes on: less depression, social phobia, anxiety, and aggression, and more relationship satisfaction and social support.[7] The proud also have higher self-esteem, which itself has a few things going for it (greater happiness, for one).[8]

This is an impressive list, but a rather obvious one. It probably doesn't surprise you that people who feel good about particular achievements also feel good about other things (themselves more generally, for example) and are happier, less depressed, and so on. So rather than ponder the obvious, I want instead to focus on some of the less blatant boons of pride, some of the things that may not occur to you and may not have occurred to Vidal.

By definition, pride follows success. You do well on an exam, you feel proud; you close a deal with an important client, and you feel proud. Hard work, struggle, and achievement come first; pride comes later. But does the causal river ever flow in the other direction? Does pride ever *cause* success?

Although I haven't mentioned it yet, you might have correctly guessed that pride is an emotion. And when we social psychologists want to study how emotions work, we bring people into the lab, manipulate their feelings, and then sit back and watch what happens. There are many ways to induce emotions in the lab: Ask participants to remember and relive a emotional experience, read a sad or funny story, watch a scary film clip, or maybe even pose an emotional facial expression. And like many good experimental manipulations in social psychology, emotion inductions usually involve lying to participants just a little.

Lisa Williams, a psychologist at the University of New South Wales, and David DeSteno of Northeastern University did a bit of this kind of lying in one of their studies.[9] Subjects came into the lab and were told that they'd be doing some visual perception and mental rotation tasks. (This part was actually true.) The first exercise was a dot estimation task. This is exactly what it sounds like: See an array of multicolored dots, guess how many red dots there are. Participants did this ten times.

After the dot task, participants were led to believe that the experimenter was off calculating their dot-estimation performance scores. A little while later, the experimenter came back into the room with the following news for some of the participants: "You received a score of 124 out of 147, which is the ninety-fourth percentile. Great job on that! That's one of the highest scores we've seen so far!" Now, this part of the story was a lie. None of the feedback was true. In fact, this was the pride manipulation. These participants hadn't really done well at all; they were just a random group of subjects assigned to the pride condition. To really sell the manipulation, the experimenter put on a little show while delivering the feedback, acting rather impressed by the subject's masterly dot-estimating skills, smiling and gesticulating, and intoning her admiration into every word.

Other participants in the experiment were exposed to none of this: They weren't told anything at all about their performance; no scores, no percentiles, and no smiling or gesticulation. This was the control condition.

Next came the mental rotation exercise: a long and tedious task in which subjects had to judge whether pairs of 3-D figures were composed of two identical figures, one of the pair simply a rotated version of the other. This task actually measures visuo-spatial cognition, but Williams and DeSteno weren't interested in this. All they cared about was how long people would persist with this mundane activity. They told participants that they could work on the task for as long as they liked and that there was no obligation to finish it.

The question of interest: do the proud persist longer than controls? We know that pride often follows hard work, but does it also induce it?

The answer: yes.

Proud participants spent about seven minutes working on the task. Control participants, who received no smiling, gesticulating pride inducement, could stomach it for only five minutes.

Now, this might all seem rather contrived to you, manipulating emotions in a laboratory and seeing what comes of it. And it's true that the lab contexts in which we run our studies often lack some of the complexity of the "real world." But don't concern yourself too much. The same thing happens in the very real-world context of Dutch insurance companies.

Willem Verbeke of Erasmus University in Rotterdam had a group of insurance salespeople imagine that they'd performed well at work, had been praised by their bosses and colleagues, and even had their successes applauded in the company newsletter.[10] Later, when these same people were asked about their work habits, those who felt more pride about their imagined success showed more adaptive sales behavior and reported working harder.

So pride makes us persevere both inside and outside the lab. But why?

Emotions, remember, are complex and multidimensional things—a rich blend of the physiological, experiential, behavioral, and cognitive. It is this last component, the cognitive dimension, that turns out to be particularly important in understanding the workings of pride. Put simply, pride changes the way we behave because it changes the way we think.

Mary Herrald and Joe Tomaka, of the University of Texas at El Paso, brought participants into their Health Psychophysiology Lab to do a social interaction task.[11] This involved chatting with an experimenter about their opinions on college-related topics (e.g., "Do you prefer large or small classes and why?"). While doing this task, some people got a pride manipulation. As in Williams and DeSteno's study, this involved bogus performance feedback: "You're doing a lot better than the other students" and "You're doing great; you brought up a lot of interesting points."

All the while, participants were being videotaped. Once the study was over, the researchers had independent judges code the videotaped interactions for how well participants performed. And, no surprises here, just as in Williams and DeSteno's study, proud subjects did better than controls (who received no praise during the task). Once again, pride improved performance. But why?

To answer this, Herrald and Tomaka went one step further. To get some insight into *why* the proud were better performers, they also asked participants what they were thinking just after the task. Subjects rated their agreement with the following statements: "I am responsible for how well things are going," "I am very satisfied with what I am accomplishing," and "Things are turning out well because of what I'm doing." These statements measure feelings of control. They measure the extent to which success is a product of one's own actions. And just as the researchers expected, the proud agreed with these statements more than those who received no pride inducement. Pride changed the way that participants thought about the situation. The proud believed that it was their own actions that brought about success, and these feelings of efficacy and control improved performance.

These results hint at the self-reinforcing nature of pride. Achievement breeds pride, which in turn changes the way we think, giving us a greater sense of confidence and control, which in turn makes us persevere, increasing the chances of further success and thus further pride. The emotion feeds off itself by encouraging cognitive shifts and behavioral changes that increase the likelihood of future successes.

Pride and Leadership

Pride and leadership; chicken and egg. Do the proud lead, ascending through the ranks on the confidence that their successes have brought them? Or do leaders later, through their achievements, become proud? It's probably a little of both, but the only way we can really know is to go back into the lab.

Consider another experiment by Lisa Williams and David DeSteno.[12]

You and another participant come into a lab. You are met there by an experimenter and a third participant. The three of you are told that this study is about vision and spatial ability. You will do a series of tasks in which you will have to mentally rotate objects, blah, blah, blah (yes, that old story).

The experimenter then takes the three of you off to separate rooms to give you an eye test, the results of which will be used to calibrate some of the other tasks in the experiment.

You then all come back to the central space and sit around a large table. On the table is a cube, something like a Rubik's cube, a puzzle that the experimenter proceeds to unwind into a long rod with little cubes protruding from it. The task: spend six minutes working as a team, twisting and bending the rod back into cube form. It's a mental rotation exercise.

This is what the experiment looked like to the participants. But as you might be starting to guess, things in this study weren't all above board.

First, there were in fact only two real participants: you and the person you arrived with. The third, already waiting at the lab, was a confederate, there to make up numbers in the group task.

Second, surprise, surprise, the eye test had nothing to do with the calibration of other tasks. This was the pride manipulation. Just as in Williams and DeSteno's pride and perseverance study, some participants got the "you're better than ninety-four percent of others" routine, whereas others, the controls, got no feedback.

This time, Williams and DeSteno were interested in how proud participants would act in the group puzzle-solving task. So they filmed the puzzle-solving sessions and later coded the length of time each person spent working on the puzzle. The confederate was told beforehand to play with the puzzle for about one minute. This left five minutes to be split between the proud participants and their partners (who received no emotional boost). And did the proud chicken lay the leadership egg? Did the proud adopt leadership roles?

Yes. Participants in the pride condition spent about a minute longer working on the puzzle than did the control participants.

(It's important to note that, from a methodological perspective, the effects were due specifically to feelings of *pride*, not just positive mood. Doing well on a test may make one proud, but it also generally puts one in a good mood. To really implicate pride in these effects, Williams and DeSteno had to control for general positive feelings. When they did, it was clear that pride was doing all the work here.)

This fits nicely with the perseverance work. Pride induces feelings of self-confidence and control, which promote effort and even success. And this *I think I can* mind-set nudges people toward taking the lead in a group activity.

But Are They Liked?

All this is fine, but you may be thinking that the real problem with the proud is that no one really likes them. Sure they persevere and lead, but they may be reviled for their achievements. Just as no one likes a know-it-all, few may warm to an achieve-it-all. It's not that the proud don't get the job done; they do, as the studies covered previously show us. The problem is that others might get a little resentful of these high achievers. But what does the research say? Are the proud liked or disliked?

To answer this we can take another look at Williams and DeSteno's leadership study.[13] Recall that after doing the eye test, which served as the pride manipulation, participants did the group puzzle-solving task. Following this exercise, participants rated their impressions of the other people in the group. Each answered questions like, "Did you perceive your partners as having high ability?" "How much did they contribute?" "How dominant were they?" When these ratings were combined and analyzed, perhaps not surprisingly, people in the pride condition were perceived as more dominant.

Of course, this makes perfect sense given that proud participants took the lead on the puzzle task. But the interesting question is: Were the proud liked? Well, Williams and DeSteno's subjects liked the proud just fine, rating them as significantly more likable than controls and confederates. And this fits with other work by Jessica Tracy and her colleagues, which shows that people who tend to experience pride—of the authentic variety, that is—have higher relationship satisfaction and social support, suggesting that they are quite popular with others.[14] So, far from being social pariahs, the proud are actually quite attractive. We not only recognize their abilities and their leadership tendencies, we like them all the more for them.

Is Altruistic Pride an Oxymoron?

As one of the so-called self-conscious emotions, pride might be excused for being rather preoccupied with the self. Can pride ever benefit others?

In 1995, the Midlife in United States survey, conducted by the MacArthur Foundation Research Network on Successful Midlife Development, shone a psychological spotlight on forty-eight of America's fifty states.[15]

Among other questions, the participants telephoned for the survey were asked to rate their agreement with the following statement: "When I think about the work I do in the community, I feel a good deal of pride."

They were also asked about their charitable behaviors: Did

they spend any time volunteering, and if so, where? Was this work health related or school related, political, or something altogether different?

Daniel Hart of Rutgers University and M. Kyle Matsuba of the University of Missouri at St. Louis took this survey data and considered how feelings of pride were related to charity work.[16] If the proud are the selfish, conceited, arrogant jerks that some believe them to be, then we would expect pride to be linked with lower volunteerism rates. In fact, the exact opposite was the case: The more pride people took in the work they did for their communities, the more hours of volunteer work they reported doing. Impressively, this was true even when accounting for personality factors that might influence both pride and volunteering. Regardless of how friendly or agreeable people were, the more pride they felt, the more charity work they did.

How to BIRG

Despite all the good that can come from pride, there is one obvious downside: In order to feel it, you have to first experience success, which usually means being good at something, or at least being willing to work rather hard. This may come as unwelcome news to many (especially those prone to that other deadly sin, sloth). But take heart, sloths: Thankfully, for those of us too lazy to do any of the hard work ourselves, there's a loophole.

During the 1973 collegiate football season, Robert Cialdini, then assistant professor of psychology at Arizona State University, and a group of his colleagues visited seven colleges in the United States.[17] From Ohio State to Notre Dame, from Michigan to Pittsburgh, Cialdini's colleagues were a fixture at introductory psychology classes. Each Monday during the football season Cialdini had confederates monitor the fashion quirks of intro psych students. Of particular interest: were students wearing the college colors to class? Were Notre Damers donning Fighting Irish T-shirts? Were Ohio State students wearing the red and white of the Buckeyes?

But Cialdini was interested not just in *what* these students were wearing but also in *when* they were wearing it. The pertinent question: were college colors more likely to make an appearance in Monday's psychology class if the university's football team had won on the weekend?

Cialdini's study was based on the idea that people happily take pride not only in what they themselves do, but also in what others do. It's in this sense that parents are proud of their children and we, as Australians or Americans, for example, are proud of our troops. When others who are in some way similar to us do well, we happily take some of the credit.

So did this kind of vicarious pride show itself in freshmen fashion? It certainly did. Students tended to flaunt their college affiliations more after their team had a win than after they had a loss. Moreover, the larger the margin of victory, the greater the number of students flying the proverbial college flag.

What we have here is what Cialdini called BIRGing: basking in reflected glory. And it's not just sports teams that are the targets of BIRGing. After Barack Obama won the 2008 presidential election, Obama supporters kept their yard signs up for about five days postelection; McCain supporters took theirs down after only three.[18]

Why do people do it? To feel better about themselves, of course. In studies following up his college football demonstration, Cialdini showed that people tend to BIRG in an attempt to secure esteem in the eyes of others. Using a variety of experimental techniques, he found that people who were made to feel bad about themselves subsequently claimed greater affiliation with a winning team. Allowing the halo of similar, successful others to cast some light our way makes us feel a little better about ourselves.

The advice here is straightforward: If you can't beat them, identify with those who can, and BIRG.

The Myths and Realities of Narcissus

We have considered authentic pride up to this point; now let's turn to the bad kind: hubris. This, remember, is the arrogant and conceited pride that fancies itself a little too much. It comes about when one attributes success not to effort, but to stable internal causes such as talent or skill or, indeed, good looks.

People inclined to hubris tend to be more aggressive, more socially phobic, and more anxious than those who aren't.[19] They also tend to have poorer relationships and feel less supported by those around them.

And, as if this list weren't bad enough, according to Claire Ashton James of the University of Groningen in the Netherlands, the hubristically proud are more prejudiced. In a paper that could only be called "Pride and Prejudice," Ashton-James and Jessica Tracy report inducing hubristic pride in participants by having them recall a time when they had "behaved in a self-important manner, or felt pretentious or stuck-up."[20] When participants were later asked to form impressions of an out-group, by rating them on traits such as "friendly" and "mean," they were more negative in their overall evaluations than were controls. (And while we're on the topic, another point in favor of authentic pride: participants induced with this good kind of pride showed no increase in prejudice.)

We can get even further insight into the nature of hubris by considering a close psychological relative: narcissism.

You probably know the myth of Narcissus, at least in broad strokes. Good-looking Greek mortal, goes down to a lake, takes one look at his reflection in the water and is hooked. He loves it. Loves it so much, in fact, that he can't bear to look away. So there he sits, lakeside, staring at his reflection until he dies of starvation (or drowns, depending on the version; either way, you get the point).

Narcissus is the embodiment of hubris. And although from the psychological point of view hubris and narcissism aren't quite the same thing, researchers consider hubris to be the emotional core of the narcissistic personality. And just like hubristic pride, narcissism looks less than virtuous at first glance.

As you might expect, the narcissist is confident, and although such confidence has its perks (most obviously, it feels good), it also has its drawbacks. Narcissists tend to perform poorly in academic contexts and also underperform in a range of tasks when performance is private.[21] When the narcissist has no audience, he won't bother trying. And just like those who tend toward hubris, narcissists also have long-term relationship difficulties, often being less liked by others.[22]

Admittedly, things don't look good. But not so fast. There is a detail of the Narcissus myth that you may not remember. After Narcissus died, the nymph Echo took pity on him and turned him into a flower: Daffodil is its English name; its botanic name—narcissus. It's true, of course, that this flower is poisonous, but still, it is rather pretty. So is there anything pleasantly floral about everyday narcissism?

Yes, according to an extensive review by W. Keith Campbell

and Laura Buffardi, psychologists at the University of Georgia.[23] Although narcissists perform poorly in some instances, if performance is tied to an opportunity to self-enhance, they do remarkably well. And although they may get into relationship difficulties in the long run, the attractiveness of their confidence and charm ensures that narcissists are successful in initiating relationships.

So the story of hubris and narcissism is a little more complicated than that of authentic pride. There are downsides—more aggression and anxiety and relationship troubles—but there are also positives. Narcissists persist and their charm often pays off. Even this kind of pride isn't always so bad.

We have up until now been looking at pride from the *inside*. We have considered what it is like to experience the sin, how this experience changes our thinking, and how these mental shifts change our behavior.

But the story from the inside is only half the story. To get a full understanding of what pride does for us, we need to take at look at this emotion from the *outside*. We need to consider the functions not of *experiencing* pride but of *expressing* it. And to do this, we need to turn, naturally, to the judo tournament of the 2004 Olympic Games.

Pride's True Reflection

It's not often that scientists turn to the martial arts for answers to the big questions, but it does happen. At the judo competition of the 2004 Olympic Games, Jessica Tracy and fellow emotions researcher David Matsumoto, from San Francisco State University, had an official photographer for the International Judo Federation take pictures of athletes both during and right after each match.[24]

Snapping with shutter speeds of up to 1/500th of a second, the photographer produced moment-to-moment records of each judoka's reactions to winning or losing a bout. Once all the photos were in, Tracy and Matsumoto had them coded by trained raters. They were interested in whether or not each photo contained evidence of the following:

1. Head tilted back (about 20°)
2. Smile
3. Arms out or raised
4. Hands clenched into fists
5. Chest expanded
6. Torso out

Why? Because this is what pride looks like. In previous work, Tracy had shown that people everywhere, from North American college students, to the inhabitants of isolated rural settlements in Burkina Faso, to four-year-old kids, consistently classify people displaying these markers as expressing pride.[25] This near universal recognition of pride was, by the way, a remarkable finding in itself. Although researchers had for some time acknowledged that so-called basic emotions (anger, fear, happiness, sadness, disgust, and surprise) have universally recognizable expressions, no one had really considered pride a candidate for widespread recognition.

What Tracy and Matsumoto were expecting in the judo study was that pride's head tilts and expanded chests and the like would be expressed more so after a win than after a loss. This seems a rather obvious prediction, and indeed they found what they expected: All six of the pride markers were displayed more often after a win.

But things get particularly interesting when you consider that they did the exact same study with blind athletes at the Paralympics. Judo has been a fixture at the Paralympic Summer Games since 1988. The rules are similar to sighted judo and the competition format is much the same. Again, the researchers had a photographer chronicle the moment-to-moment reactions of winners and losers. And, remarkably, even athletes blind from birth showed a consistent pride display after a win. These athletes couldn't have learned the display via visual cues, of course, which lends weight to the notion that the pride expression is innate.

This finding is particularly striking because it, along with the fact that people all over the world recognize the emotion, suggests that pride may have developed to serve a particular evolutionary function. Like other emotions, pride communicates. From an evolutionary perspective, emotions are not only feelings (the inside angle), they are also nonverbal messages to others (the outside angle). When you see an angry face, you know you'd better walk the other way or get ready for a fight. And much like the snarl of anger or the raised eyebrows of surprise, the expanded chest and arms akimbo display of pride says something specific about the expresser. It says simply: *I'm successful, I'm high-status.* Had the judges at the Paralympics been confused about whom to give the gold medal to, they had simply to consider the angle of head tilt to be sure.

And why precisely is signaling status via the pride expression evolutionarily functional? Well, people with high status get benefits that those on the lower rungs do not. Expressing pride lets people know that you're an appropriate target for deferential treatment, respect, mates, resources, and all manner of other things that increase the chances of your passing on your genes to the next generation. If you're winning judo tournaments or bringing in big game from the hunt and no one knows about it, chances are that social approval, women, resources, and respect aren't going to come your way.

All, Even Football, Is Vanity

On June 29, 2004, New Jersey introduced the United States' first vanity tax. Writing on the tax in the *Journal of Legal Medicine*, lawyer Michael Ruel points out that what is officially known as New Jersey's Cosmetic Medical Procedure Tax is essentially a levy on any procedure aimed at improving a person's appearance without meaningfully promoting the proper functioning of the body.[26] The legalese surrounding the tax is a little obtuse, but in essence it is a levy on merely cosmetic, as opposed to medical, procedures.

And it's not just the Garden Staters who have come down hard on vanity. Minnesota and Hawaii followed suit in 2006. Arkansas tried in 2005 and failed. This raises the general question: Should people be dissuaded, via taxes or otherwise, from taking a little pride in their appearance?

The answer: not if they are quarterbacks in the National Football League (NFL).

The NFL has an intricate system for keeping track of player performance. There are team stats and defensive line stats and, of course, individual player stats. One can track the sacks and interceptions made by defensive linemen or the fumbles made by punt returners. And then, of course, there are the quarterback numbers: completions, touchdowns, first downs, yards gained . . . the list goes on.

The point of all this statistical pedantry is to track performance. The numbers tell the story. A player's worth is in his stats and, in theory, the stats should go partway, if not all the way, to determining the value of a player. The quarterback who makes passes and gains ground gets paid. End of story.

Well, not quite. The story is actually a little more complicated than this, according to David J. Berri, an economist from Southern Utah University.[27] Berri and some of his colleagues were interested in whether there was anything more to player value (read: "player salaries") than objective performance.

To do this, they began with headshots of 312 NFL quarterbacks taken between 1995 and 2006. They fed these into a program called Symmeter, which measured the facial symmetry of each quarterback. They then predicted salaries from symmetry (which, as you may have guessed, is a measure of attractiveness: symmetrical = attractive) as well as a bunch of objective measures of performance, including previous season's passing yards, career pass attempts, and Pro Bowl status.

As expected, the objective measures predicted salaries: More passes and more Pro Bowls mean more money. But so did attractiveness. Over and above the impact of a range of statistical measures of performance, players with more symmetrical faces were better paid. In fact, a player with a symmetry score of one standard deviation above the mean (that is, a score higher than 84 percent of others), gets paid 12.8 percent more than an average-looking quarterback.

So pretty quarterbacks get more money. But such effects aren't restricted to the football field. At school, homely-looking kids gets get poorer grades than their attractive classmates.[28] And in the workplace there is a similar "plainness penalty": The most homely get paid up to 10 percent less than those of average looks.[29] (That's in the United States. In the United Kingdom and

Australia, the plainness penalty is at least twice as big.)[30] Plus, if that's not unfair enough, the uglier you are, the more likely you are to turn to crime.[31]

Some other benefits of being attractive: more dating experience, more sexual experiences, better physical and mental health, more occupational success, more popularity, more self-confidence, and better social skills.[32]

Of course, a lot of the positive consequences of beauty stem from what other people will do for you if you have a pretty face. Attractive kids get better grades in large part because teachers favor the good-looking. Even strangers will do the beautiful a good turn. If you're easy on the eyes, people will sign your petitions, give you directions, run errands for you, give you money for a tetanus shot, and, of interest to social psychologists, participate in your studies.[33]

You may have detected a sleight of hand in all this talk about attractiveness. *Does he really expect me to believe that beauty and vanity are the same thing?* No, I don't. But I had to make the point clear: As much as we'd like it not to be true, the beautiful score breaks in life that the rest of us just don't have.

Now back to vanity. Despite what our mothers say, not all of us are beautiful. But this needn't condemn us to a life of general misery and incompetence, poor social skills, tetanus, and unsigned petitions. With a little work (and I don't just mean of the surgical kind), the rest of us can also cash in on the attractiveness halo. We may not be able to easily alter our facial symmetry, but we can put vanity to work for us. We can comb our hair and clean our teeth and polish our shoes, maybe add a little lipstick or straighten our ties.

Because yes, grooming matters. And it may even trump natural good looks. Michael French, a sociologist from the University of Miami, and some of his colleagues made the most of a large data set based on about twenty thousand adolescents' responses to various interview questions about health and school and related topics.[34] What French was interested in was the impact of personal appearance on academic performance at high school. As expected, he found that physical attractiveness (measured by interviewers' ratings of interviewees) predicted grade-point average.

At first glance, the results seem to tell the familiar story: Beauty brings benefits. But an interesting (and comforting) pattern of results emerges when you look at the data more carefully. When French took grooming into account, he found that the effects of physical attractiveness per se disappeared.

Another important point to note is that vanity is not just about the face. It's also about clothes, and thankfully, shirts and dresses are a little easier to change than faces.

Our clothes go a long way to defining us. Entire identities are tied to a leather jacket, a bolo tie, or a Stetson. But clothes not only constitute identity, they also communicate it. An outfit or even a single piece of clothing can tell others anything from what music we like to where we're from or where we work.

Samuel Gosling, a social psychologist from the University of Texas at Austin, has spent the better part of the last decade carefully studying the messages encoded in people's possessions, their walks, and their clothes.

He can tell you that people with inspirational posters on their bedroom walls are neurotic, that people who swing their arms when they walk are extroverted, and that those with uncluttered offices are conscientious.[35]

On the sartorial front there are the following encryptions: dark clothes = neurotic; formal dress = conscientious; messy and unconventional clothing = open to new things; cleavage and expensive clothes = narcissism, at least in women (male cleavage signals something altogether different).[36]

But clothes have a mystical power beyond constituting and communicating identities. They are persuasive signals, and while they may not entirely maketh the man, they do maketh the men (and women) around one change their behaviors in interesting ways.

Imagine standing at a set of traffic lights waiting to cross the street. Next to you stands a young man, about thirty, wearing a freshly pressed suit, white shirt, and polished shoes. The walk signal flashes Don't Walk but the young man crosses anyway. So you ask yourself the question: to jaywalk or not to jaywalk? When Monroe Lefkowitz, Robert Blake, and Jane Mouton of the University of Texas staged this exact scenario in the commercial district of Austin, they found an interesting pattern of results attesting to the persuasive power of clothing.[37] When their confederate was dressed in the high-status attire of suit, shirt, and shiny shoes, 14 percent of unwitting participants (pedestrians who just happened to be standing at the lights at the time) jaywalked when the confederate did. But when the confederate was dressed in the low-status getup of scuffed shoes, dirty pants, and denim shirt, only 4 percent of participants followed him across the street.

The unpleasant fact is this: The way we look matters. Our faces, our bodies, our skin, our clothes. All these things make a difference in how we are perceived and what we can achieve. And while a little pride in appearance probably can't get you from a lowly "1" to a perfect "10," it might, via a primp here and a straighten there, get you a better grade in school or help ward off tetanus.

Salman Rushdie and Christopher Hitchens used to play a word game that involved coming up with book titles that never quite hit the presses: *The Big Gatsby, Good Expectations*, and *Mr. Zhivago* were some of the favorites.[38] Equally unpoetic and flat, but no-where near as witty: *Prides and Prejudice*. Second-rate, but rather apt, given what actually happens in Austen's novel. Elizabeth Bennet slides back and forth between love and hate for Mr. Darcy, alternately admiring his honor (read: authentic pride) and loathing his conceitedness (read: hubris).

There are two prides in Austen's novel, just as there are two prides in the work of social psychologists. Austen touches on some of the goods of pride, but misses others that have since come to light through the work of scientists. The proud work hard and achieve; they take the lead and are liked.

Still, she sees the big picture. There are two kinds of pride, and the key to making the most of this queen of the deadly sins is to indulge the good and resist (at least for the most part) the bad. And if you want to get good grades and have strangers give you money, a little pride in your appearance can't hurt either.

CONCLUSION

Just When You Thought
There Were Only Seven . . .

s I was writing this book, *BBC Focus* magazine reported a
worldwide survey that ranked the world's most sinful countries.[1] Using metrics similar to those used by Thomas Vought
and colleagues in their mapping of US sins—theft statistics for
envy, BMI for gluttony, number of sick days for sloth—the BBC
compiled the following list of winners:

Lust: South Korea
Gluttony: United States
Greed: Mexico
Sloth: Iceland
Anger: South Africa
Envy: Australia
Pride: Iceland

With just a hint of pride (the authentic variety, of course), I'm
happy to say that, overall, Australia was deemed the world's most

sinful nation. I do feel sorry for those who came close—the United States in second place and Canada third—and sorrier still for those that didn't make the list at all (Greenland, anybody?). But virtuous Greenlanders and those like them need not worry, for it seems that there might be other ways to take the mantle of "world's most sinful."

On March 9, 2008, Bishop Gianfranco Girotti, the Regent of the Apostolic Penitentiary, one of the most important tribunals in the Roman Catholic Church, revamped the seven deadly sins for the new millennium. In an interview with the Vatican newspaper *l'Osservatore Romano*, Bishop Girotti added various "social" sins such as drug use, abortion, pollution, and stem-cell research to the traditional, and hopefully now familiar, seven: "You offend God not only by stealing, blaspheming or coveting your neighbor's wife, but also by ruining the environment, carrying out morally debatable scientific experiments, or allowing genetic manipulations which alter DNA or compromise embryos."[2]

And it's not only the odd Regent of the Apostolic Penitentiary that has taken a shot at updating the list of deadlies for the twenty-first century. According to a 2005 BBC survey, a contemporary list of deadly sins would read:[3]

Cruelty
Adultery
Bigotry
Dishonesty
Hypocrisy
Greed
Selfishness

Not to belabor the point (and not to miss the point that the BBC poll was somewhat tongue-in-cheek), but the label "sin" (and the related notion that certain behaviors are uniformly bad) does nothing but render complex psychological and social phenomena simplistically unidimensional. Greed you've already heard about. Dishonesty, categorically bad? How about hypocrisy? Haven't you ever tried a little innocuous dissembling to spare someone's feelings? "How do I look in this dress, darling?"

There is no doubt that for some, explicit guidance from respected authorities provides a much-needed moral compass in a complex world. Indeed, the ability to judge a behavior as black or white, as obviously right or wrong, does simplify life quite a bit. But as we've seen with the traditional deadly sins, the reality is much more complex. Simplistic categorization of social and psychological phenomena into "sins" and "virtues," into the "good" and the "bad," strips human action of its inherent and fascinating richness. What's more, it marginalizes "sinners" and hampers serious and sophisticated discourse.

What strikes you as a more sensible course of action? Reasoned and informed debate about the ethical consequences of stem-cell research, or simply asserting that such research is a sin and abandoning it all together? Drug treatment programs based on careful consideration of the scientific evidence surrounding the distal and proximal causes of drug abuse, or a "drug abuse = sin" mantra, which condemns drug users not only to an eternity in hell, but to social exclusion and stigmatization?

You have seen throughout this book that seven psychological characteristics of the human species that have for about sixteen centuries been demonized as mortally sinful are in fact rather good for us. All it takes to get to this conclusion is a little careful thought, a perusal of the scientific record, and a willingness to abandon a cultural legacy that drastically simplifies human nature. If you take a moment, it's not difficult to see how lust, gluttony, greed, sloth, anger, envy, and pride can often work for you and for those around you. And if you take just a few moments more, you'll find it an equally reasonable proposition that almost any facet of human behavior—from genetic engineering to selfishness—is too complex, too multifaceted, and in the end often simply too functional to be given the label "sin."

ACKNOWLEDGMENTS

Thanks (in no particular order) to all who have helped shape this book. For reading bits of the manuscript, thanks to Bill von Hippel, Ladd Wheeler, Jessica Tracy, Jessica Payne, Nick Haslam, Peter Kuppens, Pete Koval, Omri Gillath, Bianca Levis, and Hanne Watkins. Special thanks to Cordelia Fine and Cassie Govan.

Thanks also to Barbara Loewenstein and Norman Kurz at Loewenstein and Associates and to Heather Lazare and everyone else at Three Rivers Press.

For their support, thanks to Mum and Dad, Nick, Lizzie, Clare, and Matt (and many others). Most of all, thanks to Stacey.

NOTES

Introduction

1. Thomas Vought, Ryan Bergstrom, Michael Dulin, and Mitchell Stimers, "The Spatial Distribution of the Seven Deadly Sins by County Within the United States" (poster presented at the Annual Meeting of the Association of American Geographers, Las Vegas, NV, 2009).
2. S. Gregory the Great, *Morals on the Book of Job* (London: F. & J. Rivington, 590/1847).
3. Rebecca DeYoung, *Glittering Vices* (Grand Rapids, MI: Baker Publishing Group, 2009).
4. William Sinnott-Armstrong, ed., *Moral Psychology*, vol. 1, *The Evolution of Morality* (Cambridge, MA: MIT Press, 2008).
5. William Hoverd and Chris Sibley, "Immoral Bodies: The Implicit Association Between Moral Discourse and the Body," *Journal for the Scientific Study of Religion* 46 (2007): 391–403.
6. S. Gregory the Great, *Morals on the Book of Job*.

Chapter 1. Lust

1. Cindy M. Meston and David M. Buss, "Why Humans Have Sex," *Archives of Sexual Behavior* 36 (2007): 477–507.
2. D. Amen, "Bedtime Stories," *Men's Health* 19, no. 2 (2005): 152.
3. "Cosmo's Sex Trick Hall of Fame," *Cosmopolitan* 238, no. 6 (2005): 118.
4. David M. Buss, "Sex Differences in Human Mate Preferences: Evo-

lutionary Hypotheses Tested in 37 Cultures," *Behavioral and Brain Sciences* 12 (1989): 1–49; David M. Buss, *The Evolution of Desire: Strategies of Human Mating* (New York: Basic Books, 1994); David M. Buss and David R. Schmitt, "Sexual Strategies Theory: An Evolutionary Perspective on Human Mating," *Psychological Review* 100 (1993): 204–232; Boguslaw Pawlowski and Slawomir Koziel, "The Impact of Traits Offered in Personal Advertisements on Response Rates," *Evolution and Human Behavior* 23 (2002): 139–149.

5. Buss, *The Evolution of Desire.*

6. Jeffrey A. Hall, Namkee Park, Hayeon Song, and Michael J. Cody, "Strategic Misrepresentation in Online Dating: The Effects of Gender, Self-Monitoring, and Personality Traits," *Journal of Social and Personal Relationships* 27 (2010): 117–135.

7. James R. Roney, "Effects of Visual Exposure to the Opposite Sex: Cognitive Aspects of Mate Attraction in Human Males," *Personality and Social Psychology Bulletin* 29 (March 2003): 393–404.

8. Bruce J. Ellis and Donald Symons, "Sex Differences in Sexual Fantasy: An Evolutionary Psychological Approach," *Journal of Sex Research* 27 (November 1990): 527–555.

9. Antonio Zadra, "Sex Dreams: What Do Men and Women Dream About?" *Sleep* 20 (2007): A376.

10. Russell D. Clark III and Elaine Hatfield, "Gender Differences in Receptivity to Sexual Offers," *Journal of Psychology and Human Sexuality* 2 (1989): 39–55.

11. Buss, *The Evolution of Desire.*

12. Meston and Buss, "Why Humans Have Sex."

13. Willibrord Weijmar Schultz, Pek van Andel, Ida Sabelis, and Eduard Mooyaart, "Magnetic Resonance Imaging of Male and Female Genitals During Coitus and Female Sexual Arousal," *British Medical Journal* 319 (1999): 1596–1600.

14. Omri Gillath, Mario Mikulincer, Gurit E. Birnbaum, and Phillip R. Shaver, "Does Subliminal Exposure to Sexual Stimuli Have the Same Effects on Men and Women?" *Journal of Sex Research* 44 (2007): 111–121.

15. Jon K. Maner, Douglas T. Kenrick, D. Vaughn Becker, Theresa E. Robertson, Brian Hofer, Steven L. Neuberg, Andrew W. Delton, Jonathan Butner, and Mark Schaller, "Functional Projection: How Fundamental Social Motives Can Bias Interpersonal Perception," *Journal of Personality and Social Psychology* 88 (2005): 63–78.

16. Walter Stephan, Ellen Berscheid, and Elaine Walster, "Sexual Arousal and Heterosexual Perception," *Journal of Personality and Social Psychology* 20 (1971): 93–101; Jon K. Maner, Matthew T. Gailliot, D. Aaron Rouby, and Saul L. Miller, "Can't Take My Eyes Off You: Attentional Adhesion to Mates and Rivals," *Journal of Personality and Social Psychology* 93 (2007): 389–401.

17. Gregory J. Madden and Warren K. Bickel, *Impulsivity: The Behavioral and Neurological Science of Discounting* (Washington, DC: American Psychological Association, 2010)

18. Bram van den Bergh, Siegfried Dewitte, and Luk Warlop, "Bikinis Instigate Generalized Impatience in Intertemporal Choice," *Journal of Consumer Research* 35 (June 2008): 85–97.

19. Ibid.

20. Richard E. Nisbett, Kaiping Peng, Incheol Choi, and Ara Norenzayan, "Culture and Systems of Thought: Holistic Versus Analytic Cognition," *Psychological Review* 108 (2001): 291–310.

21. Jens Förster, Amina Özelsel, and Kai Epstude, "How Love and Lust Change People's Perception of Relationship Partners," *Journal of Experimental Social Psychology* 46 (2010): 237–246.

22. Jens Förster, Kai Epstude, and Amina Özelsel, "Why Love Has Wings and Sex Has Not: How Reminders of Love and Sex Influence

Creative and Analytic Thinking," *Personality and Social Psychology Bulletin* 35 (2009): 1479–1490.

23. Omri Gillath, "Neural and Cognitive Correlates of Exposure to Sex" (talk presented at the 22nd annual meeting of the Association for *Psychological Science*, Boston, MA, May 2010).

24. Brad J. Bushman, "Violence and Sex in Television Programs Do Not Sell Products in Advertisements," *Psychological Science* 16 (2005): 702–708.

25. Anemone Cerridwen and Dean Keith Simonton, "Sex Doesn't Sell—Nor Impress! Content, Box Office, Critics, and Awards in Mainstream Cinema," *Psychology of Aesthetics, Creativity, and the Arts* 3 (2009): 200–210.

26. Vladas Griskevicius, Noah J. Goldstein, Chad R. Mortensen, Robert B. Cialdini, and Douglas T. Kenrick, "Going Along Versus Going Alone: When Fundamental Motives Facilitate Strategic (Non) Conformity," *Journal of Personality and Social Psychology* 91 (2006): 281–294.

27. Vladas Griskevicius, Joshua M. Tybur, Jill M. Sundie, Robert B. Cialdini, Geoffrey F. Miller, and Douglas T. Kenrick, "Blatant Benevolence and Conspicuous Consumption: When Romantic Motives Elicit Strategic Costly Signals," *Journal of Personality and Social Psychology* 93 (2007): 85–102.

28. Ibid.

29. Omri Gillath, Mario Mikulincer, Gurit E. Birnbaum, and Phillip R. Shaver, "When Sex Primes Love: Subliminal Sexual Priming Motivates Relationship Goal Pursuit," *Personality and Social Psychology Bulletin* 34 (2008): 1057–1069.

30. Ibid.

31. Dan Ariely and George Loewenstein, "The Heat of the Moment:

The Effect of Sexual Arousal on Sexual Decision Making," *Journal of Behavioral Decision Making* 19 (2006): 87–98.

32. Richard Ronay and William von Hippel, "The Presence of an Attractive Woman Elevates Testosterone and Physical Risk Taking in Young Men," *Social Psychological and Personality Science* 1 (January 2010): 57–64.

33. Geoffrey F. Miller, "Sexual Selection for Moral Virtues," *Quarterly Review of Biology* 82 (2007): 97–125.

34. David M. Buss and Michael Barnes, "Preferences in Human Mate Selection," *Journal of Personality and Social Psychology* 50 (1986): 559–570.

35. Vladas Griskevicius, Robert B. Cialdini, and Douglas T. Kenrick, "Peacocks, Picasso, and Parental Investment: The Effects of Romantic Motives on Creativity," *Journal of Personality and Social Psychology* 91 (2006): 63–76.

36. Miller, "Sexual Selection for Moral Virtues."

37. Griskevicius et al., "Blatant Benevolence and Conspicuous Consumption."

38. *Catechism of the Catholic Church* (Homebush, NSW: St Pauls, 1994).

Chapter 2. Gluttony

1. P. Rozin, C. Fischler, S. Imada, A. Sarubin, and A. Wrzesniewski, "Attitudes to Food and the Role of Food in Life in the U.S.A., Japan, Flemish Belgium and France: Possible Implications for the Diet-Health Debate," *Appetite* 33 (1999): 163–180; Paul Rozin, "The Meaning of Food in Our Lives: A Cross-Cultural Perspective on Eating and Well-Being," *Journal of Nutrition Education and Behavior* 37 (2005): S107–S112.

2. National Center for Health Statistics, National Health and Nutrition

Examination Survey: Data Tables, retrievcd December 31, 2010, http://www.cdc.gov/nchs/data/nhanes/databriefs/adultweight .pdf; Paul Rozin, Kimberly Kabnick, Erin Pete, Claude Fischler, and Christy Shields, "The Ecology of Eating: Smaller Portion Sizes in France Than in the United States Help Explain the French Paradox," *Psychological Science* 14 (September 2003): 450–454.

3. Susan E. Hill, "The Ooze of Gluttony: Attitudes Towards Food, Eating, and Excess in the Middle Ages," in *The Seven Deadly Sins: From Communities to Individuals*, ed. Richard Newhauser (The Netherlands: Koninklijke Brill NV, 2007).

4. Richard I. Stein and Carol J. Nemeroff, "Moral Overtones of Food: Judgments of Others Based on What They Eat," *Personality and Social Psychology Bulletin* 21 (May 1995): 480–490.

5. Ibid.

6. Sarah-Jeanne Salvy, Julie C. Bowker, Lauren A. Nitecki, Melissa A. Kluczynski, Lisa J. Germeroth, and James N. Roemmich, "Impact of Simulated Ostracism on Overweight and Normal-Weight Youths' Motivation to Eat and Food Intake," *Appetite* 56 (February 2011): 39–45.

7. Brian Wansink, "Can Package Size Accelerate Usage Volume?" *Journal of Marketing* 60 (July 1996): 1–14; Brian Wansink and Junyong Kim, "Bad Popcorn in Big Buckets: Portion Size Can Influence Intake as Much as Taste," *Journal of Nutrition Education and Behavior* 37 (2005): 242–245.

8. Brian Wansink, "Environmental Factors That Increase the Food Intake and Consumption Volume of Unknowing Consumers," *Annual Review of Nutrition* 24 (2004): 455–479.

9. Brian Wansink, James E. Painter, and Jill North, "Bottomless Bowls: Why Visual Cues of Portion Size May Influence Intake," *Obesity Research* 13 (2005): 93–100.

10. Brian Wansink and Koert Van Ittersum, "Bottoms Up! The Influ-

ence of Elongation on Pouring and Consumption Volume," *Journal of Consumer Research* 30 (2003): 455–463.

11. For more on the ice cream study, see Brian Wansink, Koert van Ittersum, and James E. Painter, "Ice Cream Illusions: Bowls, Spoons, and Self-Served Portion Sizes," *American Journal of Preventive Medicine* 31 (2006): 240–243; on office candy consumption, see B. Wansink, J. E. Painter, and Y.-K. Lee, "The Office Candy Dish: Proximity's Influence on Estimated and Actual Consumption," *International Journal of Obesity* 30 (2006): 871–875; on M&M colors, see Barbara E. Kahn and Brian Wansink, "The Influence of Assortment Structure on Perceived Variety and Consumption Quantities," *Journal of Consumer Research* 30 (2004): 519–533.

12.

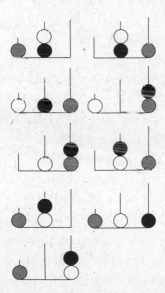

13. Michael W. Green and Peter J. Rogers, "Impairments in Working Memory Associated with Spontaneous Dieting Behaviour," *Psychological Medicine* 28 (1998): 1063–1070.

14. Ibid.

15. Matthew T. Gailliot, "Unlocking the Energy Dynamics of Executive Functioning," *Perspectives on Psychological Science* 3 (2008):
245–263.

16. Matthew T. Gailliot, Roy F. Baumeister, C. Nathan DeWall, Jon
K. Maner, E. Ashby Plant, Dianne M. Tice, Lauren E. Brewer,
and Brandon J. Schmeichel, "Self-Control Relies on Glucose as a
Limited Energy Source: Willpower Is More Than a Metaphor,"
Journal of Personality and Social Psychology 92 (2007): 325–336.

17. Matthew T. Gailliot and Roy F. Baumeister, "The Physiology of
Willpower: Linking Blood Glucose to Self-Control," *Personality
and Social Psychology Review* 11 (2007): 303–327; Gailliot, "Unlocking the Energy Dynamics of Executive Functioning."

18. Matthew T. Gailliot, B. Michelle Peruche, E. Ashby Plant, and
Roy F. Baumeister, "Stereotypes and Prejudice in the Blood: Su-
crose Drinks Reduce Prejudice and Stereotyping," *Journal of Experimental Social Psychology* 45 (2009): 288–290.

19. Barbara Briers, Mario Pandelaere, Siegfried Dewitte, and Luk
Warlop, "Hungry for Money: The Desire for Caloric Resources
Increases the Desire for Financial Resources and Vice Versa,"
Psychological Science 17 (2006): 939–943.

20. Hans C. Breiter, Itzhak Aharon, Daniel Kahneman, Anders Dale,
and Peter Shizgal, "Functional Imaging of Neural Responses to
Expectancy and Experience of Monetary Gains and Losses," *Neuron* 30 (May 2001): 619–639; John P. O'Doherty, Ralf Diechmann,
Hugo D. Critchley, and Raymond J. Dolan, "Neural Responses
During Anticipation of a Primary Taste Reward," *Neuron* 33, no.
28 (2001): 815–826.

21. Briers et al., "Hungry for Money."

22. The impact of labels was reported in Brian Wansink, Koert van

Ittersum, and James E. Painter, "How Diet and Health Labels Influence Taste and Satiation," *Journal of Food Science* 69 (2004): S340–S346; the preferences for wine and chocolate cake were discussed in Brian Wansink, *Mindless Eating: Why We Eat More Than We Think* (New York: Bantam Dell, 2007).

23. Akshay R. Rao and Kent B. Monroe, "The Effect of Price, Brand Name, and Store Name on Buyers' Perceptions of Product Quality: An Integrative Review," *Journal of Marketing Research* 26 (August 1989): 351–357.

24. Hilke Plassmann, John O'Doherty, Baba Shiv, and Antonio Rangel, "Marketing Actions Can Modulate Neural Representations of Experienced Pleasantness," *Proceedings of the National Academy of Sciences* 105 (January 2008): 1050–1054.

25. Aner Sela, Jonah Berger, and Wendy Liu, "Variety, Vice, and Virtue: How Assortment Size Influences Option Choice," *Journal of Consumer Research* 35 (April 2009): 941–951.

26. Sheena S. Iyengar and Mark R. Lepper, "When Choice Is Demotivating: Can One Desire Too Much of a Good Thing?" *Journal of Personality and Social Psychology* 79 (2000): 995–1006.

27. Dan Ariely and Jonathan Levav, "Sequential Choice in Group Settings: Taking the Road Less Traveled and Less Enjoyed," *Journal of Consumer Research* 27 (December 2000): 279–290.

28. Rozin et al., "Attitudes to Food and the Role of Food in Life."

29. Rozin et al., "The Ecology of Eating."

30. Ibid.

31. Wansink, *Mindless Eating.*

32. Richard Wrangham, *Catching Fire: How Cooking Made Us Human* (London: Profile Books, 2009).

33. Matthew W. Gillman, Sheryl L. Rifas-Shiman, A. Lindsay Frazier, Helaine R. H. Rockett, Carlos A. Camargo Jr., Alison E.

Field, Catherine S. Berkey, and Graham A. Colditz, "Family Dinner and Diet Quality Among Older Children and Adolescents," *Archives of Family Medicine* 9 (March 2000): 235–240.

34. *Oxford English Dictionary Online*, s.v. "companion, n/1," retrieved January 1, 2011, http://www.oed.com:80/Entry/37402.

Chapter 3. Greed

1. "Memorable Quotes for Wall Street," Internet Movie Database, http://www.imdb.com/title/tt0094291/quotes, retrieved January 4, 2011.
2. Betsey Stevenson and Justin Wolfers, "Economic Growth and Subjective Well-Being: Reassessing the Easterlin Paradox," *Brookings Papers on Economic Activity*, Spring 2008, 1–87.
3. Ibid., 65–67.
4. Aristotle, "The Politics," in *Aristotle: The Politics and the Constitution of Athens*, ed. S. Everson and trans. J. Barnes (Cambridge, England: Cambridge University Press, 1996), 9–207, 185, 197.
5. Leaf Van Boven and Thomas Gilovich, "To Do or to Have? That Is the Question," *Journal of Personality and Social Psychology* 85 (2003): 1193–1202.
6. Ibid.
7. Daniel Gilbert, *Stumbling on Happiness* (London: Harper Perennial, 2006).
8. Ibid.
9. Ed Diener and Robert Biswas-Diener, *Happiness: Unlocking the Mysteries of Psychological Wealth* (Malden, MA: Blackwell, 2008).
10. Ibid.
11. Ed Diener and Martin Seligman, "Beyond Money: Toward an Economy of Well-Being," *Psychological Science in the Public Interest* 5 (2004): 1–31.
12. Diener and Biswas-Diener, *Happiness*.

13. Ibid.

14. Thomas Gilovich, Robert Vallone, and Amos Tversky, "The Hot Hand in Basketball: On the Misperception of Random Sequences," *Cognitive Psychology* 17 (1985): 295–314.

15. Todd McFall, Charles Knoeber, and Walter Thurman, "Contests, Grand Prizes and the Hot Hand," *Journal of Sports Economics* 10 (2009): 236–255.

16. Douglas Jenkins Jr., Atul Mitra, Nina Gupta, and Jason Shaw, "Are Financial Incentives Related to Performance? A Meta-analytic Review of Empirical Research," *Journal of Applied Psychology* 83 (1998): 777–787.

17. Edward L. Deci, "Effects of Externally Mediated Rewards on Intrinsic Motivation," *Journal of Personality and Social Psychology* 18 (1971): 105–115.

18. Philip Tetlock, Orie Kristel, Beth Elson, Melanie Green, and Jennifer Lerner, "The Psychology of the Unthinkable: Taboo Tradeoffs, Forbidden Base Rates, and Heretical Counterfactuals," *Journal of Personality and Social Psychology* 78 (2000): 853–870.

19. Dan Ariely, *Predictably Irrational* (London: HarperCollins, 2008).

20. Uri Gneezy and Aldo Rustichini, "Pay Enough or Don't Pay at All," *Quarterly Journal of Economics*, August 2000, 791–810.

21. Kathleen Vohs, Nicole Mead, and Miranda Goode, "Psychological Consequences of Money," *Science* 314 (2006): 1154–1156.

22.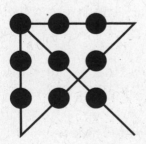

Kathleen Vohs, Nicole Mead, and Miranda Goode, "Merely Activating the Concept of Money Changes Personal and Interpersonal Behavior," *Current Directions in Psychological Science* 17 (2008): 209.

23. Ibid.

24. Xinyue Zhou, Kathleen Vohs, and Roy Baumeister, "The Symbolic Power of Money: Reminders of Money Alter Social Distress and Physical Pain," *Psychological Science* 20 (2009): 700–706.

25. Kathleen Vohs, "Small Reminders of Money Elicit Big Changes in Behavior" (keynote address at 39th Annual Conference of the Society of Australasian Social Psychologists, Melbourne, Australia, 2009).

26. Kathleen Vohs, Nicole Mead, and Miranda Goode, "Psychological Consequences of Money," *Science* 314 (2006): 1154–1156.

27. Ibid.

28. Stephen Lea and Paul Webley, "Money as Tool, Money as Drug: The Biological Psychology of a Strong Incentive," *Behavioral and Brain Sciences* 29 (2006): 161–209.

Chapter 4. Sloth

1. *Oxford English Dictionary Online*, s.v. "sloth," retrieved December 29, 2010, http://www.oed.com:80/Entry/182099.

2. Robert E. Sinkewicz, *Evagrius of Pontus: The Greek Ascetic Corpus* (Oxford: Oxford University Press, 2006), 99.

3. Max Weber, *The Protestant Ethic and the "Spirit" of Capitalism and Other Writings* (New York: Penguin Books, 2002).

4. Bertrand Russell, *In Praise of Idleness* (London: Allen & Unwin, 1935), 12.

5. Robert Louis Stevenson, "An Apology for Idlers," 1876, retrieved from http://essays.quotidiana.org/stevenson/apology_for_idlers/.

6. Sheldon Cohen, William J. Doyle, Cuneyt M. Alper, Denise Janicki-Deverts, and Ronald B. Turner, "Sleep Habits and Susceptibility to the Common Cold," *Archives of Internal Medicine* 169 (2009): 62–67.

7. Matthew P. Walker and Robert Stickgold, "Sleep, Memory and Plasticity," *Annual Review of Psychology* 57 (2006): 139–166.

8. Jessica D. Payne, Daniel L. Schacter, Ruth E. Propper, Li-Wen Huang, Erin J. Wamsley, Matthew A. Tucker, Matthew P. Walker, and Robert Stickgold, "The Role of Sleep in False Memory Formation," *Neurobiology of Learning and Memory* 92 (2009): 327–334.

9. Ibid.

10. Jessica D. Payne and Elizabeth A Kensinger, "Sleep's Role in the Consolidation of Emotional Episodic Memories," *Current Directions in Psychological Science* 19 (2010): 290–295.

11. Walker and Stickgold, "Sleep, Memory and Plasticity."

12. Ullrich Wagner, Steffen Gais, Hilde Haider, Rolf Verleger, and Jan Born, "Sleep Inspires Insight," *Nature* 427 (2004): 352–355.

13. Denise J. Cai, Sarnoff A. Mednick, Elizabeth M. Harrison, Jennifer C. Kanady, and Sara C. Mednick, "REM, Not Incubation, Improves Creativity by Priming Associative Networks," *Proceedings of the National Academy of Sciences of the United States of America* 106 (2009): 10130–10134.

14. Erin J. Wamsley, Matthew Tucker, Jessica D. Payne, Joseph A. Benavides, and Robert Stickgold, "Dreaming of a Learning Task is Associated with Enhanced Sleep-Dependent Memory Consolidation," *Current Biology* 20 (2010): 850–855.

15. Ibid.

16. Jonathan Schooler, Erik Reichle, and David Halpern, "Zoning Out While Reading: Evidence for Dissociations Between Experience and Metaconsciousness," in *Thinking and Seeing: Visual Metacognition in*

Adults and Children, ed. Daniel Levin (Cambridge, MA: MIT Press, 2004), 203–226.

17. Eric Klinger and Miles Cox, "Dimensions of Thought Flow in Everyday Life," *Imagination, Cognition, and Personality* 7 (1987–1988): 105–128.

18. Deborah F. Greenwald and David W. Harder, "Fantasies, Coping Behavior, and Psychopathology," *Journal of Clinical Psychology* 59 (October 2003): 1089–1095.

19. John Kounios, Jennifer L. Frymiare, Edward M. Bowden, Jessica I. Fleck, Karuna Subramaniam, Todd B. Parrish, and Mark Jung-Beeman, "The Prepared Mind: Neural Activity Prior to Problem Presentation Predicts Subsequent Solution by Sudden Insight," *Psychological Science* 17 (2006): 882–890.

20. Kalina Christoff, Alan M. Gordon, Jonathan Smallwood, Rachelle Smith, and Jonathan W. Schooler, "Experience Sampling during fMRI Reveals Default Network and Executive System Contributions to Mind Wandering," *Proceedings of the National Academy of Sciences of the United States of America* 106 (2009): 8719–8724.

21. Malia F. Mason, Michael I. Norton, John D. Van Horn, Daniel M. Wegner, Scott T. Grafton, and C. Neil Macrae, "Wandering Minds: The Default Network and Stimulus-Independent Thought," *Science* 315 (2007): 393–395.

22. Jackie Andrade, "What Does Doodling Do?" *Applied Cognitive Psychology* 24 (2010): 100–106.

23. K. Anders Ericsson, Ralf Th. Krampe, and Clemens Tesch-Romer, "The Role of Deliberate Practice in the Acquisition of Expert Performance," *Psychological Review* 100 (1993): 363–406; Malcolm Gladwell, *Outliers: The Story of Success* (New York: Little, Brown / Hachette Book Group, 2008).

24. Nicholas O. Rule and Nalini Ambady, "The Face of Success: Inferences from Chief Executive Officers' Appearance Predict Company Profits," *Psychological Science* 19 (2008): 109–111.

25. Timothy D. Wilson and Jonathan W. Schooler, "Thinking Too Much: Introspection Can Reduce the Quality of Preferences and Decisions," *Journal of Personality and Social Psychology* 60 (1991): 181–192.

26. Ap Dijksterhuis, Rick. B van Baaren, Karin C.A. Bongers, Maarten W. Bos, Matthijs L. van Lecuwen, and Andries van der Leij, "The Rational Unconscious: Conscious Versus Unconscious Thought in Complex Consumer Choice," *Social Psychology of Consumer Behavior*, ed. Michaela Wanke (2009) 468–477.

27. Ibid.

28. Ap Dijksterhuis and Loran F. Nordgren, "A Theory of Unconscious Thought," *Perspectives on Psychological Science* 1 (2006): 95–109.

29. Ben R. Newell, Kwan Yao Wong, Jeremy C. H. Cheung, and Tim Rakow, "Think, Blink or Sleep on It? The Impact of Modes of Thought on Complex Decision Making," *Quarterly Journal of Experimental Psychology* 62 (2009): 707–732; John W. Payne, Adriana Samper, James R. Bettman, and Mary Frances Luce, "Boundary Conditions on Unconscious Thought in Complex Decision Making," *Psychological Science* 19 (2008): 1118–1123.

30. Dijksterhuis et al., "The Rational Unconscious."

31. Jaap Ham, Kees van den Bos, and Evert A. Van Doorn, "Lady Justice Thinks Unconsciously: Unconscious Thought Can Lead to More Accurate Justice Judgments," *Social Cognition* 27 (2009): 509–521.

32. John A. Bargh, Mark Chen, and Lara Burrows, "Automaticity of Social Behavior: Direct Effects of Trait Construct and Stereotype Activation on Action," *Journal of Personality and Social Psychology* 71 (1996): 230–244.

33. Rob Gray and Russ Branaghan, "Changing Driver Behavior Through Unconscious Stereotype Activation," in *Proceedings of the Fifth International Driving Symposium on Human Factors in Driver Assessment, Training and Vehicle Design* (2009).

34. Robert Levine, *A Geography of Time* (New York: Basic Books, 1997).

35. Ibid.

36. Robert V. Levine, Karen Lynch, Kunitate Miyake, and Marty Lucia, "The Type A City: Coronary Heart Disease and the Pace of Life," *Journal of Behavioral Medicine* 12 (1989): 509–524.

37. Robert V. Levine, Stephen Reysen, and Ellen Ganz, "The Kindness of Strangers Revisited: A Comparison of 24 US Cities," *Social Indicators Research* 85 (2008): 461–481.

38. Levine et al., "The Type A City."

39. John M. Darley and C. Daniel Batson, "From Jerusalem to Jericho: A Study of Situational and Dispositional Variables in Helping Behavior," *Journal of Personality and Social Psychology* 27 (1973): 100–108.

40. Ibid., 101.

41. Ibid., 102.

42. Stanley Milgram, "The Experience of Living in Cities," *Science* 167 (March 1970): 1461–1468.

43. Ibid.

Chapter 5. Anger

1. *Oxford English Dictionary Online*, s.v. "violence, n," retrieved December 29, 2010, http://www.oed.com:80/Entry/223638.

2. Joel R. Davitz, *The Language of Emotion* (New York: Academic Press, 1969).

3. Jill Lobbestael, Arnoud Arntz, and Reinout W. Wiers, "How to Push Someone's Buttons: A Comparison of Four Anger-Induction Methods," *Cognition and Emotion* 22 (2008): 353–373.

4. The first estimate is from Howard Kassinove, Denis G. Sukhodolsky, Sergei V. Tsytsarev, and Svetlana Solovyova, "Self-Reported Anger Episodes in Russia and America," *Journal of Social Behavior and Personality* 12 (1997); 301–324; the second from H. Meltzer, "Student's Adjustments in Anger," *Journal of Social Psychology* 4 (August 1933): 285–309.

5. Evidence of cardiovascular problems is reported in Janice E. Williams, Catherine C. Paton, Ilene C. Siegler, Marsha L. Eigenbrodt, F. Javier Nieto, and Herman A. Tyroler, "Anger Proneness Predicts Coronary Heart Disease Risk: Prospective Analysis from the Atherosclerosis Risk in Communities (ARIC) Study," *Circulation* 101 (May 2000): 2034–2039; Patricia P. Chang, Daniel E. Ford, Lucy A. Meoni, Nae-Yuh Wang, and Michael J. Klag, "Anger in Young Men and Subsequent Premature Cardiovascular Disease: The Precursors Study," *Archives of Internal Medicine* 162 (2002): 901–906. Other risk factors are noted in Jerry L. Deffenbacher, Maureen E. Huff, Rebekah S. Lynch, Eugene R. Oetting, and Natalie F. Salvatore, "Characteristics and Treatment of High-Anger Drivers," *Journal of Counseling Psychology* 47 (2000): 5–17.

6. Mario Mikulincer, "Reactance and Helplessness Following Exposure to Unsolvable Problems: The Effects of Attributional Style," *Journal of Personality and Social Psychology* 54 (1988): 679–686.

7. Michael Cosio, "Soda Pop Vending Machine Injuries," *Journal of the American Medical Association* 260 (1988): 2697–2699.

8. Charles S. Carver and Eddie Harmon-Jones, "Anger Is an Approach-Related Affect: Evidence and Implications," *Psychological Bulletin* 135 (2009): 183–204.

9. Ibid.

10. Maya Tamir, Christopher Mitchell, and James J. Gross, "Hedonic and Instrumental Motives in Anger Regulation," *Psychological Science* 19 (2008): 324–328.

11. Brett Q. Ford, Maya Tamir, Tad T. Brunyé, William R. Shirer, Caroline R. Mahoney, and Holly A. Taylor, "Keeping Your Eyes on the Prize: Anger and Visual Attention to Threats and Rewards," *Psychological Science* 21 (2010): 1098–1105.

12. John Cassian, *The Institutes of the Coenobia, and the Remedies for the Eight Principal Vices*, trans. Boniface Ramsey, OP, in *Ancient Christian Writers*, vol. 58 (Mahwah, NJ: Newman Press, 2000).

13. Norbert Schwarz and Gerald L. Clore, "Mood, Misattribution, and Judgments of Well-Being: Informative and Directive Functions of Affective States," *Journal of Personality and Social Psychology* 45 (1983): 513–523.

14. Jennifer S. Lerner and Dacher Keltner, "Fear, Anger, and Risk," *Journal of Personality and Social Psychology* 81 (2001): 146–159.

15. Maia J. Young, Larissa Z. Tiedens, Heajung Jung, and Ming-Hong Tsai, "Mad Enough to See the Other Side: Anger and the Search for Disconfirming Information," *Cognition and Emotion* 25 (2011): 10–21.

16. Ibid.

17. Wesley G. Moons and Diane M. Mackie, "Thinking Straight While Seeing Red: The Influence of Anger on Information Processing," *Personality and Social Psychology Bulletin* 33 (2007): 706–720.

18. Joseph Henrich, Steven J. Heine, and Ara Norenzayan, "The Weirdest People in the World," *Behavioral and Brain Sciences* 33 (2010): 61–83.

19. Jonathan Haidt, "The New Synthesis in Moral Psychology," *Science* 316 (2007): 998–1002; Jonathan Haidt and Jesse Graham, "When Morality Opposes Justice: Conservatives Have Moral Intuitions That Liberals May Not Recognize," *Social Justice Research* 20 (March 2007): 98–116.

20. Haidt and Graham, ibid.

21. Henrich, Heine, and Norenzayan, "The Weirdest People in the World."

22. Jonathan Haidt, "The Emotional Dog and Its Rational Tail: A Social Intuitionist Approach to Moral Judgment," *Psychological Review* 108 (2001): 814–834; Paul Rozin, Laura Lowery, Sumio Imada, and Jonathan Haidt, "The CAD Triad Hypothesis: A Mapping Between Three Moral Emotions (Contempt, Anger, Disgust) and Three Moral Codes (Community, Autonomy, Divinity)," *Journal of Personality and Social Psychology* 76 (1999): 574–586.

23. Roberto Gutierrez and Roger Giner-Sorolla, "Anger, Disgust, and Presumption of Harm as Reactions to Taboo-Breaking Behaviors," *Emotion* 7 (2007): 853–868.

24. Joydeep Srivastava, Francine Espinoza, and Alexander Fedorikhin, "Coupling and Decoupling of Unfairness and Anger in Ultimatum Bargaining," *Journal of Behavioral Decision Making* 22 (2009): 475–489.

25. Larissa Z. Tiedens, "Anger and Advancement Versus Sadness and Subjugation: The Effect of Negative Emotion Expressions of Social Status Conferral," *Journal of Personality and Social Psychology* 80 (2001): 86–94.

26. Ibid.

27. Ibid.

28. Adam Nagourney, "Calling Senator Clinton 'Angry,' G.O.P. Chairman Attacks," *New York Times*, February 5, 2006, A16.

29. Maureen Dowd, "Who's Hormonal? Hillary or Dick?" *New York Times*, February 8, 2006, A21.

30. Victoria L. Brescoll and Eric Luis Uhlmann, "Can an Angry Woman Get Ahead? Status Conferral, Gender, and Expression of Emotion in the Workplace," *Psychological Science* 19 (2008): 268–275.

31. Gerben A. van Kleef, Carsten K. W. De Dreu, and Antony S. R. Manstead, "The Interpersonal Effects of Anger and Happiness in Negotiations," *Journal of Personality and Social Psychology* 86 (2004): 57–76.

32. Marwan Sinaceur and Larissa Z. Tiedens, "Get Mad and Get More Than Even: When and Why Anger Expression Is Effective in Negotiations," *Journal of Experimental Social Psychology* 42 (2006): 314–322.

33. Gerben A. van Kleef and Stéphane Côté, "Expressing Anger in Conflict: When It Helps and When It Hurts," *Journal of Applied Psychology* 92 (2007): 1557–1569.

34. Hajo Adam, Aiwa Shirako, and William W. Maddux, "Cultural Variance in the Interpersonal Effects of Anger in Negotiations," *Psychological Science* 21 (2010): 882–889.

35. James R. Averill, "Studies on Anger and Aggression: Implications for Theories of Emotion," *American Psychologist* 38 (November 1983): 1145–1160; Howard Kassinove, et al., "Self-Reported Anger Episodes in Russia and America," *Journal of Social Behavior and Personality* 12 (1997): 301–324.

36. Kassinove et al., "Self-Reported Anger Episodes in Russia and America"; Raymond Chip Tafrate, Howard Kassinove, and Louis Dundin, "Anger Episodes in High- and Low-Trait-Anger Community Adults," *Journal of Clinical Psychology* 58 (2002): 1573–1590.

37. Kassinove et al., "Self-Reported Anger Episodes in Russia and America."

38. Tafrate, Kassinove, and Dundin, "Anger Episodes in High- and Low-Trait-Anger Community Adults."

39. Mary Gordon, "Anger," in *Deadly Sins*, ed. Thomas Pynchon (New York: William Morrow, 1993).

Chapter 6. Envy

1. W. Gerrod Parrott and Richard H. Smith, "Distinguishing the Experiences of Envy and Jealousy," *Journal of Personality and Social Psychology* 64 (1993): 906–920

2. Leon Festinger, "A Theory of Social Comparison Processes," *Human Relations* 7 (1954): 117–140.

3. Francis Bacon, "Of Envy," *The Essays* (London: Penguin Group, 1985), 83–87.

4. Daniel T. Gilbert, Kathryn A. Morris, and R. Brian Giesler, "When Comparisons Arise," *Journal of Personality and Social Psychology* 69 (1995): 227–236.

5. Lisa G. Aspinwall and Shelley E. Taylor, "Effects of Social Comparison Direction, Threat, and Self-Esteem on Affect, Self-Evaluation, and Expected Success," *Journal of Personality and Social Psychology* 64 (1993): 708–722.

6. Ladd Wheeler, "Motivation as a Determinant of Upward Comparison," Supplement 1, *Journal of Experimental Social Psychology* (1966): 27–31.

7. Penelope Lockwood and Ziva Kunda, "Superstars and Me: Predicting the Impact of Role Models on the Self," *Journal of Personality and Social Psychology* 73 (1997): 91–103.

8. George Loewenstein, "Anticipation and the Valuation of Delayed Consumption," *Economic Journal* 97 (September 1987): 666–684.

9. Ibid.

10. Richard H. Smith and Sung Hee Kim, "Comprehending Envy," *Psychological Bulletin* 133 (2007). 46–64.

11. Camille S. Johnson and Diederik A. Stapel, "No Pain, No Gain: The Conditions Under Which Upward Comparisons Lead to Better Performance," *Journal of Personality and Social Psychology* 92 (2007): 1051–1067.

12. Hart Blanton, Bram P. Buunk, Frederick X. Gibbons, and Hans Kuyper, "When Better-Than-Others Compare Upward: Choice of Comparison and Comparative Evaluation as Independent Predictors of Academic Performance," *Journal of Personality and Social Psychology* 76 (1999): 420–430.

13. John J. Seta, "The Impact of Comparison Processes on Coactors' Task Performance," *Journal of Personality and Social Psychology* 42

(1982): 281–291; David M. Marx and Jasmin S. Roman, "Female Role Models: Protecting Women's Math Test Performance," *Personality and Social Psychology Bulletin* 28 (2002): 1183–1193.

14. Naomi Mandel, Petia K. Petrova, and Robert B. Cialdini, "Images of Success and the Preference for Luxury Brands," *Journal of Consumer Psychology* 16 (2006): 57–69.

15. Lockwood and Kunda, "Superstars and Me."

16. Ibid.

17. Timothy D. Wilson, Thalia Wheatley, Jonathan M. Meyers, Daniel T. Gilbert, and Danny Axsom, "Focalism: A Source of Durability Bias in Affective Forecasting," *Journal of Personality and Social Psychology* 78 (2000): 821–836.

18. Philip Brickman, Dan Coates, and Ronnie Janoff-Bulman, "Lottery Winners and Accident Victims: Is Happiness Relative?" *Journal of Personality and Social Psychology* 36 (1978): 917–927.

19. Richard E. Lucas and Andrew E. Clark, "Do People Really Adapt to Marriage?" *Journal of Happiness Studies* 7 (2006): 405–426; Richard E. Lucas, Andrew E. Clark, Yannis Georgellis, and Ed Diener, "Reexamining Adaptation and the Set Point Model of Happiness: Reactions to Changes in Marital Status," *Journal of Personality and Social Psychology* 84 (2003): 527–539.

20. Jaime L. Kurtz, Timothy D. Wilson, and Daniel T. Gilbert, "Quantity Versus Uncertainty: When Winning One Prize Is Better Than Winning Two," *Journal of Experimental Social Psychology* 43 (2007): 979–985.

21. Timothy Wilson, Jay Meyers, and Daniel Gilbert, "'How Happy Was I, Anyway?' A Retrospective Impact Bias," *Social Cognition* 21 (2003): 407–432.

22. Timothy Wilson, David Centerbar, Deborah Kermer, and Daniel Gilbert, "The Pleasures of Uncertainty: Prolonging Positive Moods

in Ways People Do Not Anticipate," *Journal of Personality and Social Psychology* 88 (2005): 5–21.

23. Douglas H. Wedell and Allen Parducci, "The Category Effect in Social Judgment: Experimental Ratings of Happiness," *Journal of Personality and Social Psychology* 55 (1988): 341–356.

24. Christopher K. Hsee, Reid Hastie, and Jingqiu Chen, "Hedonomics: Bridging Decision Research with Happiness Research," *Perspectives on Psychological Science* 3 (2008): 224–243.

25. Christopher K. Hsee, Yang Yang, Naihe Li, and Luxi Shen, "Wealth, Warmth, and Well-Being: Whether Happiness Is Relative or Absolute Depends on Whether It Is About Money, Acquisition, or Consumption," *Journal of Marketing Research* 46 (2009): 396–409.

26. Ibid.

Chapter 7. Pride

1. Stanford M. Lyman, *The Seven Deadly Sins: Society and Evil*, rev. ed. (Dix Hills, NY: General Hall, 1989), 136; Michael Eric Dyson, *Pride: The Seven Deadly Sins* (New York: Oxford University Press, 2006); Matthew Baasten, *Pride According to Pope Gregory the Great: A Study of the Moralia* (Lewiston, NY: Edwin Mellen Press, 1986).

2. Jessica L. Tracy and Richard W. Robins, "The Psychological Structure of Pride: A Tale of Two Facets," *Journal of Personality and Social Psychology* 92 (2007): 506–525.

3. Aristotle, *The Ethics of Aristotle: The Nicomachean Ethics* (New York: Viking, 1955).

4. Tracy and Robins, "The Psychological Structure of Pride."

5. Martin Amis, *The Moronic Inferno* (London: Jonathan Cape, 1986), 105.

6. Gore Vidal, "Pride," in *Deadly Sins*, ed. Thomas Pynchon (New York: William Morrow, 1993), 67.

7. Jessica L. Tracy, Azim F. Shariff, and Joey T. Cheng, "A Naturalist's View of Pride," *Emotion Review* 2 (April 2010): 163–177.

8. Roy F. Baumeister, Jennifer D. Campbell, Joachim I. Krueger, and Kathleen D. Vohs, "Does High Self-Esteem Cause Better Performance, Interpersonal Success, Happiness or Healthier Lifestyles?" *Psychological Science in the Public Interest* 4 (May 2003): 1–44.

9. Lisa A. Williams and David DeSteno, "Pride and Perseverance: The Motivational Role of Pride," *Journal of Personality and Social Psychology* 94 (2008): 1007–1017.

10. Willem Verbeke, Frank Belschak, and Richard P. Bagozzi, "The Adaptive Consequences of Pride in Personal Selling," *Journal of the Academy of Marketing Science* 32 (2004): 386–402.

11. Mary M. Herrald and Joe Tomaka, "Patterns of Emotion-Specific Appraisal, Coping, and Cardiovascular Reactivity During an Ongoing Emotional Episode," *Journal of Personality and Social Psychology* 83 (2002): 434–450.

12. Lisa A. Williams and David DeSteno, "Pride: Adaptive Social Emotion or Seventh Sin?" *Psychological Science* 20 (2009): 284–288.

13. Ibid.

14. Jessica L. Tracy, Joey T. Cheng, Richard W. Robins, and Kali H. Trzesniewski, "Authentic and Hubristic Pride: The Affective Core of Self-Esteem and Narcissism," *Self and Identity* 8 (2009): 196–213.

15. MacArthur Foundation Research Network on Successful Midlife Development, *Midlife in the United States: A National Study of Health and Well-Being* (1994–1995).

16. Daniel Hart and M. Kyle Matsuba, "The Development of Pride and Moral Life," in *The Self-Conscious Emotions: Theory and Research*, eds. Jessica L. Tracy, Richard W. Robins, and June Price Tangney (New York: Guilford Press, 2007), 114–133.

17. Robert B. Cialdini, Richard J. Borden, Avril Thorne, Marcus Randall

Walker, Stephen Freeman, and Lloyd Reynolds Sloan, "Basking in Reflected Glory: Three (Football) Field Studies," *Journal of Personality and Social Psychology* 34 (1976): 366–375.

18. Chris B. Miller, "Yes We Did! Basking in Reflected Glory and Cutting Off Reflected Failure in the 2008 Presidential Election," *Analyses of Social Issues and Public Policy* 9 (2009): 283–296.

19. Tracy et al., "Authentic and Hubristic Pride."

20. Claire E. Ashton-James and Jessica L. Tracy, "Pride and Prejudice: How Feelings About the Self Influence Judgments of Others," manuscript submitted for publication.

21. W. Keith Campbell and Laura E. Buffardi, "The Lure of the Noisy Ego: Narcissism as a Social Trap," in *Quieting the Ego: Psychological Benefits of Transcending Egotism*, eds. J. Bauer and H. Wayment (Washington, DC: American Psychological Association, 2008), 23–32.

22. Ibid.

23. Ibid.

24. Jessica L. Tracy and David Matsumoto, "The Spontaneous Expression of Pride and Shame: Evidence for Biologically Innate Nonverbal Displays," *Proceedings of the National Academy of Sciences of the United States of America* 105 (2008): 11655–11660.

25. Jessica L. Tracy and Richard W. Robins, "Show Your Pride: Evidence for a Discrete Emotion Expression," *Psychological Science* 15 (2004): 194–197; Jessica L. Tracy, Richard W. Robins, and Kristin H. Lagattuta, "Can Children Recognize the Pride Expression?" *Emotion* 5 (2005): 251–257; Jessica L. Tracy and Richard W. Robins, "The Nonverbal Expression of Pride: Evidence for Cross-Cultural Recognition," *Journal of Personality and Social Psychology* 94 (2008): 516–530.

26. Michael D. Ruel, "Vanity Tax: How New Jersey Has Opened Pandora's Box by Elevating Its Moral Judgment About Cosmetic Surgery

Without Consideration of Fair Health Care Policy," *Journal of Legal Medicine* 28 (2007): 119–134.

27. David J. Berri, Rob Simmons, Jennifer Van Gilder, and Lisle O'Neill, "What Does It Mean to Find the Face of the Franchise? Physical Attractiveness and the Evaluation of Athletic Performance" (paper presented at Western Economic Association International 85th Annual Conference, Portland, June 29 to July 3, 2010).

28. Vicki Ritts, Miles L. Patterson, and Mark E. Tubbs, "Expectations, Impressions, and Judgments of Physically Attractive Students: A Review," *Review of Educational Research* 62 (1992): 413–426.

29. Daniel S. Hamermesh and Jeff E. Biddle, "Beauty and the Labor Market," *American Economic Review* 84 (2004): 1174–1194.

30. Ibid.

31. Naci Mocan and Erdal Tekin, "Ugly Criminals," *Review of Economics and Statistics* 92 (2010): 15–30.

32. Judith Langlois, Lisa Kalakanis, Adam Rubenstein, Andrea Larson, Monica Hallam, and Monica Smoot, "Maxims or Myths of Beauty? A Meta-Analytic and Theoretical Review," *Psychological Bulletin* 126 (2000): 390–423.

33. Ibid.; Stephen West and Jan Brown, "Physical Attractiveness, the Severity of the Emergency and Helping: A Field Experiment and Interpersonal Simulation," *Journal of Experimental Social Psychology* 11 (1975): 531–538.

34. Michael T. French, Philip K. Robins, Jenny F. Homer, and Lauren M. Tapsell, "Effects of Physical Attractiveness, Personality, and Grooming on Academic Performance in High School," *Labour Economics* 16 (2009): 373–382.

35. Sam Gosling, *Snoop: What Your Stuff Says About You* (London: Profile Books, 2008).

36. Ibid.

37. Monroe Lefkowitz, Robert R. Blake, and Jane Srygley Mouton, "Status Factors in Pedestrian Violation of Traffic Signals," *Journal of Abnormal and Social Psychology* 51 (November 1955): 704–706.

38. Christopher Hitchens, *Hitch-22: A Memoir* (New York: Twelve/ Hachette Book Group, 2010).

Conclusion

1. Andy Ridgway, "The Human Brain: Hardwired to Sin," *BBC Focus* 212 (2010).

2. Nicola Gori, "The New Forms of Social Sin," *l'Osservatore Romano*, March 9, 2008.

3. Craig Brown, "Out with the Old Deadly Sins, in with the New," *Scotsman*, February 7, 2005.

ABOUT THE AUTHOR

Simon M. Laham, PhD, is an experimental social psychologist. He is currently Lecturer and Research Fellow in Psychological Sciences at the University of Melbourne, Australia. Before moving to Melbourne, Simon studied at the University of New South Wales and worked at the University of Oxford. He has published numerous academic articles on moral psychology and emotion. His popular writing has appeared in the *New Statesman*. This is his first book.

Simon blogs at themoralpsychologist.com. You can also find him at simonlaham.com.